FEELINGS

by

Terry Funnell

Feelings

Second Edition

Poems by
Terry Funnell

with
illustrations by
Peter Guest

Copyright © Terry Funnell 2000

Typeset and produced by The Hallamshire Press Limited
134 Archer Road, Sheffield S8 0JZ

Printed in Great Britain
by The Cromwell Press,
Wiltshire

British Library Cataloguing in Publication Data:

Funnell, Terry
    Feelings. – 2Rev. ed
    I. Title
    821.914

    ISBN 1-874718 05-9

Contents

Young Lovers Pass 11

My Love 13

The Graveyard 15

Springtime in the Park 16

The Stream 18

My Wish to a Teenager 19

A Father's Word 20

Armistice 22

Uncle Charlie 27

Snap 30

Kids 31

Holidays 35

The Diet 39

My Bath 40

Three Ages of Man 43

I Am Your God 43

A Sermon on the Minister 45

Searching 48

Barriers 49

A Christmas Gift 52

Just Another Tale? 55

Nativity (Yorkshire Dialect) 57

Ee! Wot a Christmas! (Yorkshire Dialect) 60

The Spirit of Christmas 66

Christmas Cards 69
Christmas 1983 71
Eyes 73
Dilemma 74
New Year 75
Poetry Lesson 1 77
Leap Year 79
A Winter's Night on the Farm 84
Not Now (A Thought of Dying) 85
Jumble 88
Football Crazy 90
Jean 92
I Might Have Been 95
Handyman 98
Neighbours 101
Scotland '88 103
A Prayer of the Heart 105
Sunday Morning 106
My Church 107
The Mountain (On Seeing Ben Nevis) 109
Santa's Lament 110
Three in a Bed 118
Feelings 121
Giving Up 122
The Hairdo 124
My Christmas Past 126
Just Another Day (A Widow's Story) 132
The Train Journey 135
Holiday Weak
    (A Little Advice from the Good Lady Wife) 140
The Car Lot 142

The Supermarket 145
Up Market 147
Ill Feelings 150
Going Green 153
Party Time 155
Welcome Home
   (A Homecoming Greeting from the Dear Wife) ... 158
At Your Service 161
Sale Away! 163
Late Kick-Off 165
The Navigator 167

Preface

Welcome to *Feelings*, the first published collection of my poems, now in its second edition and fully revised and illustrated. As an introduction (and I understand it's the done thing), I thought I'd give you a potted history of my life and times.

I was born in Sheffield in 1936, and attended St Barnabus C of E school until I was eleven, when I failed the Grammar School exam and went to Abbeydale School at Glen Road. I feel I had a good education, in spite of being an unwilling pupil for most of the time. I fell madly in love at the age of five and continued to do so every year until I met my present — and, may I say, beautiful — wife Jean. We now have three grown-up children: Jill, Bruce and Nicholas, who, over the years, have become not just family, but very dear friends.

My earliest poetic influence was my mother, whom I remember reciting poems at Church Maydays when I was a small boy — these Maydays were where I got my first taste of comic poetry. It was not until I was about twenty-five and I had kids of my own that I first put pen to paper and found that the poetry bug ran in the family. "Kids", included in this collection, must have been one of the first I wrote, purely for an audience of family and friends. People seemed to like them, and before long I was being asked to write comic verses and recite them at weddings and other gatherings, and I've just gone on from there.

My biggest influences as a young man were the poems of Marriott Edgar (remember "Albert and the Lion"?) — made famous by the great Stanley Holloway — and the radio comedian, Al Reed. What I liked about Al was his gift for spotting the humour in everyday situations, like the bloke next door or the man on the football terrace: his speciality was sending up the "Johnny Know-alls" of this world, and if you read "At Your Service" or "Football Crazy", you might just detect his influence.

As well as the humorous poems, you will find some more thoughtful reflections on life — and life gone by. I hope you find in these verses something to catch your imagination, and maybe stir *your* feelings.

I'd also like to take this opportunity to thank my son-in-law, Peter Guest, for the cartoons and my daughter, Jill Guest, who did all the original typing from my illegible scripts and sorted out the spelling into the bargain. Thanks also to the staff of Interleaf Productions for all their hard work and patience.

Terry Funnell
November 1992

YOUNG LOVERS PASS

They walked by, arm in arm tonight
And even at a glance
I saw the mystery of love
As if the angels from above
Had lit their countenance.

For in her eyes that sparkled bright
She told the world her joy,
How could she hide the love inside?
It sprang forth like a breaking tide
That no one could destroy.

The autumn leaves, crisp round their feet
Dropped gently from above,
Yet these young lovers could not see
The beauty left from every tree,
Their eyes were lost in love.

On arm in arm, and hand in hand
Their small world was complete,
She was a queen and he a king,
They made the very pathway sing
As they walked down the street.

For things around them, commonplace
Were new. Transformed at will.
And other people passing by
Recaptured all their years gone by
Remembering them still.

And for that moment I was caught
Transported with them too,
For love so sweet one cannot keep
But only as a dreamless sleep
Catch while the air is new.

I would not dash them from their peak
For once they have transcended,
They seldom show that inner glow
That only new-found lovers know
And all too soon has ended.

I could not tell these happy two
Nor could I give them reason
Why this short time of fleeting joy
They would remember like a toy
The first fruits of the season.

What joy they left with me tonight
I would that moment stay
And in their world where love is true,
And moments melt like morning dew,
Bless lovers such as they.

MY LOVE

It seems like only yesterday we met
And yet for me a day I can't forget,
He turned my world into a carousel
That must go on, I love this man so well.

The everyday no longer seems mundane,
I feel so happy, nothing can contain,
The joy within my heart, it overflows,
It is a feeling only true love knows.

What can I say? There are no words to tell
Of love like this that casts a magic spell
And leaves me floating on a higher plane
Where everything is new to see again.

Now every morning when I rise from sleep
No longer do I curse the clock and creep
Downstairs, with eyes half closed. I greet
The day with gladness, him to meet.

My heart has never known such joy before,
He has my love, I cannot give him more,
And if forever he would just be mine
Eternity would be too short a time.

O time stand still and history resign,
For more important still this love of mine,
It is more priceless too than gold or gem
My love for him a precious diadem.

And when the pen of life shall write my theme
And salad days like these are but a dream,
When time has slipped away and youth is gone
He will for me be still the only one.

THE GRAVEYARD

I wandered in one sunny afternoon
And joined the slow of foot and heavy hearted
Whose memory looked back across the years,
Whose thoughts were lost among their dear departed

The sun shone brightly on each cherished plot
And gay flowers mocked the sombre stone,
Old faces tranquil with the years,
Young faces tearfully alone.

The sentinels of stone like soldiers grey
Standing in rows, the guards of yesteryear,
What lives and loves lay hidden 'neath the earth?
What did they know of love and joy and fear?

The gravel path gives way to grass and weeds
And in a corner 'neath a hawthorn tree
A stone half covered now with twitch and grass
Reads mockingly, "Dear friend, remember me."

I hurry now, afraid to get involved,
Anxious to retrace my steps of life,
The main street bustles with the here and now
And I return to family and wife.

SPRINGTIME IN THE PARK

Come let us sing the joys of spring,
Of long and lazy days
In parks serene
Where bands are seen
Within the balustrade.

And children, fresh with eager years,
Run endless paths of green
Through gladed ways
Of summer haze
Their pretty dresses gleam.

And sombre men in morning suits
Who through the winter long
Have kept indoors
On squeaky floors
Now join the happy throng.

The river full of fishermen,
With jars and bottles held,
Gaze down with awe
On water's floor
Their noisy chatter quelled.

The swings and roundabouts and slides
Come out of hibernation,
Their colours gay
Welcome their play
Of childrens' exaltation.

Mothers with prams talk baby talk
And gather
At paths meeting,
Comparing weight and height and size
While resting on park seating.

And lovers lie on greener grass
And softer turf than many,
And lad and lass
Watch people pass
Though never seeing any.

Too busy they, each other's eyes
Are all they can enfold
On days as these
No summer breeze
Could make their love grow cold.

Give thanks for joyous summer days
And parks of recreation
Where all can share
The summer air
And pleasant relaxation.

THE STREAM

Where are you going, stranger?
On such a lovely day,
You look in such a hurry
As you dash along your way.

Why go so fast to get there?
Why not tarry for a while?
Let me look into your mirror
And reflect upon your smile.

Why do you chatter gaily
As you pass me in a trice?
Are you telling me a message
Or just giving good advice?

The world is all downhill to you
I would it were for me,
You sing a mountain waterfall
You gurgle round a tree.

The pebbles are your instrument
To play a merry tune,
You sing to serenade the sun
Or lullaby the moon.

Oh hurry on, adventurer
And do not stop or tarry,
For at your destination
You have merchant men to carry.

MY WISH TO A TEENAGER

As dawn is rising now upon your future
And endless years before you stretch away,
My wish is that you find your true ambition,
That life before you may be bright and gay.

May fun and joy and laughter be your comrades,
May happiness be yours in fullest measure,
And may you make new friends with each acquaintance,
Yet never lose the old ones that you treasure.

And when in life you stumble on the pitfalls,
May strength of purpose pull you safely through,
May courage be your armour in that moment
When Satan thinks he has a hold on you.

May all your aims be high, your thoughts be noble
May God in all His goodness be your guide,
Beneath your feet may sunshine be your pathway
As through this life, adventurous, you stride.

A FATHER'S WORD

Give me your hand
For pitfalls lie ahead,
Hold tight your grasp
To face the foes you dread.

Each step is new
Unchartered in your mind,
If I can guide
Then let me be your friend.

I travel too
Though slower is my pace,
For I have learned
Speed does not win the race.

Tread where I tread
If you see aught in me,
Let my example then
Your watchword be.

Beware of lies
That tell you black is white,
And be strong willed
When you know wrong from right.

Look for the weak,
So many need your hand,
This journey's not just yours
To seek the promised land.

I'll go so far
Then you are on your own,
Learn while you can
My journey soon is done.

Beware of fools
Who stop you on your way,
They are but sheep
And aimlessly they stray.

Your road is long,
It may be lonely too,
So mark my step
And may God walk with you.

ARMISTICE

We rose up early, Jack and I,
The sun was rising in the sky
And as the birds sang up above
I waved goodbye to my true love.

A shilling of the King we took,
Boots, gaiters and pay book,
Then donned a uniform of brown
And Jack and I went into town.

Soon we'd be sailing, he and I,
Forgetting those who'd say goodbye
And looking for adventure new
Across the sea of turquoise blue.

Jack cheered and laughed and threw his hat
For we would win, no doubt of that
While I, the quieter of the two,
Just murmured, "Yes, if we get through."

We laboured at a trench so neat
Our heads at Sergeant Newman's feet,
For he kept watch up on the top
While we dug down with all we'd got.

The day passed slowly now for Jack
And I was sick of muck and tack
And endless rain and soaking feet,
We'd gain a yard and then retreat.

When were we going to fight and win?
Where was the glory? Let's begin.
We couldn't wait to have a crack
And beat the other devils back.

Then came the orders from the Sarge:
"Come on now lads, it's up and charge."
And from our mud we climbed and clung
With bayonettes fixed up ladder rung.

Once at the top both Jack and I
Made straight for cover from the sky
We ran into a bomb hole ditch,
Our feet in water, black as pitch.

Then up again and forward thrust
We'd kill a hundred if we must,
Then Jack was parted, lost from view,
And smoke and bombs were all I knew.

I didn't know for sure while night
I'd lost my comrade in the fight,
And suddenly my zest was gone
For Jack and I were good as one.

That moment was the hell of war
For me and many gone before
Who'd lost a friend, a comrade true
Gunned down for what? We never knew.

For King and country, God and right
For freedom of a tyrant's might,
It didn't make much odds to Jack,
Just one more face not going back.

Now peaceful years have passed between
And great men say what might have been,
Generals orate the glorious past
While I begin to count the waste.

It's Armistice, that time of year
When veterans unite to hear
The words of Bishop and Lord Mayor
Uttered from the sacred books of prayer.

The flag is lowered to half mast,
The trumpet sounds a sombre blast
And balding heads are lowered again
With thoughts of Somme or Alamein.

And when it's all been said and done
And comes the moment of the gun,
Two minutes of allotted time
To think of all those comrades fine.

Then Jack comes flooding to my mind
And anecdotes of every kind,
The memories jump the years across
It's then I really count the loss.

*"And as the birds sang up above
I waved goodbye to my true love."*

The gun booms out, two minutes gone
And eyes are cleared, and noses blown,
It's over for another year
And soon the balustrades are clear.

The uniforms are put away,
The medals we wore for display
Are neatly packed in drawers again
Along with half a million men.

But thoughts are not so easy shed
And Jack still lingers in my head,
What was the cost he paid that day
A life well spent? Or thrown away?

What price the freedom I enjoy?
What price my wife? My girl, my boy?
The things I hold so dear to me?
Jack's life has bought my liberty.

Yet knowing this, I dare to say
One life is still too dear to pay,
Unless my fellow man can boast
He too will treasure freedom most.

What joy, the sense of being free,
But what a price to pay for me,
And while the years between have healed
Still poppies grow in Flanders' field.

UNCLE CHARLIE

Where has Uncle Charlie gone
Who always had a treat?
A pocket full of sweeties
When you met him in the street.

He'd a thousand different stories
Of his time beneath the sail,
And with his pipe he'd poke the air
To punctuate his tale.

He always had the time to tell
You of his mis-spent youth,
And his face was bright and open
With sincerity and truth.

And when it came to Christmas
He would dress as Santa Claus,
And at New Year, Uncle Charlie
Was the one we sent outdoors.

He'd come in with a piece of coal
and wish us all 'Good cheer',
Then he'd kiss the ladies heartily
To start the festive year.

It was always Uncle Charlie
Who would dress up at charades,
Who sang louder than the piano
And who cheated best at cards.

"And with his pipe he'd poke the air
To punctuate his tale."

Where has Uncle Charlie gone
Who made my childhood fun?
I hear he went to fight a war
That Hitler had begun.

My Uncle Charlie wasn't asked,
He volunteered to fight,
For he said, "There is no option
When a wrong confronts a right."

The parties are less noisy
Now that Uncle Charlie's gone,
The conversation's softer
And charades are not such fun.

And now I've grown, I follow paths
Where Uncle Charlie trod,
Just a man who thought of others
And who knew the love of God.

There will always be the Hitlers
To dictate their evil creed,
But it's the loving Uncle Charlies
That we desperately need.

So if you've a favourite uncle
Though his name is yet untold,
Treasure moments you are with him
For he's worth much more than gold.

SNAP

A polaroid for me .... *SNAP*
Takes instant pictures see .... *SNAP*
I'll have some fun
With everyone
Just smile this way at me .... *SNAP*

My camera's colour too .... *SNAP*
I'd love to take of you .... *SNAP*
You come out great
In any state
Don't move you're into view .... *SNAP*

I'll show you how it works .... *SNAP*
Don't give it any jerks .... *SNAP*
At just five feet
You're in a treat
Now try to smile, not smirk ..... *SNAP*

The picture's nearly done .... *SNAP*
Why do you look so dumb? ...... *SNAP*
Now time is up,
Let's have a look
Oh dear, it's of my thumb .... *SNAP*

KIDS

Oh, when you come a-knocking,
A-knocking on my door
And hear me shout, "Hang on a mo"
And wonder what it's for.
Then let me tell you, stranger,
In case you're in some doubt,
That before we let you in we have
To let some toys go out!

You could say that we're lucky
Having children by the score,
As each year passes counting heads
And finding we've one more.
But let me tell you, stranger
Before you do the same,
That each child wants to play with toys
Or dress up for a game.

For this they need a mansion
With room to run and play,
Our terraced house just has to do,
What can we parents say?
At first they start off quietly
With blackboard, chalk and duster,
But soon they tire, it's time for all
The soldiers then to muster.

Out comes the fort and indians,
The aeroplanes as well,
For in this battle, time holds out
An ancient magic spell.
The bombers bomb the cowboys
And the cowboys in reply
Load revolvers and with careful aim
Shoot bullets in the sky.

When the blood sports have all finished,
Then it's time for family games,
So prams and dolls are pulled out
And we are given different names.
For Mum and Dad are children,
And children take their place
And Golly is the dolly who must
Take the pride of place.

He's sat at table carefully
And given spoon and plate,
And woe betide the parent
Who would try to imitate.
For in the world of make believe
What does it really matter?
If there is no food upon the plate
Golly won't get any fatter.

That game has lasted long enough,
Five minutes must have gone,
So let's move on to something else
And find another one.
Now there's a place upon the floor
A shop would go quite well,
So Dad bring out the counter
While we children buy and sell.

"Now madam, what about a tin
Of beans? Or would you like
A bag of sweets? They're soiled of course,
But then you needn't bite.
Or perhaps you'd like to buy a toy?
We sell them too you know,
In fact, we'll sell you anything
For everything must go."

The shop is shut with minutes left
Before it's time for bed,
So rather than be there too soon, let's
Clean the cupboard out instead.
There's books and hooks and handbags,
Plastic balls and wooden pegs,
A teapot lid, a xylophone,
And hands and arms and legs.

For dollies that were once the rage
Of not so long ago,
Have lost their popularity
So in the cupboard go.
And then when bedtime comes around
It's up the stairs they make,
While we stride on toes between the toys
Like dancers in Swan Lake.

So when you come a-knocking
And you're minutes at the door,
Don't think that we're unfriendly
We're just trying to clear the floor.

"That game has lasted long enough,
Five minutes must have gone."

HOLIDAYS

We set off early, bright as pins,
And leave our messages behind,
"Please feed the cat and mow the lawn,
And to the budgie, please be kind.

"He's been quite poorly just of late
And needs a bit of extra care,
Oh, and Grandad, don't forget
To water all the plants out there."

Mum worries that we might have left
Some vital cargo in the hall,
And did she pack the toothbrushes,
The bucket, spade and Johnny's ball?

Well never mind, let's wave goodbye
And leave the house, the hols begun,
Although its only six o'clock
This early's never been such fun.

The open road is still in front,
Adventure's eighty miles away,
Where Mum will knit and Dad will snooze
And Jane will dig the beach away.

Who'll be the first to spot the sea?
Eight eyes observe the changing scene
And then the cry goes up, "It's there!"
Thank goodness, Johnny's looking green.

*"And did she pack the toothbrushes,
The bucket, spade and Johnny's ball?"*

*Before we go to "Sunny Lea"
Let's have two minutes on the beach,
We'll just have time to paddle too
Before the sea goes out of reach.*

*The water never seems to change,
It's just as cold as last year was,
And yet we come back every year
Because it's just like home to us.*

*Now Mrs Gordon's at the door,
The sunlight gleams upon her hair,
We all exchange the warm hellos
And plastic ham's the Sunday fare.*

*"Now here's your key" (we're trusted guests)
"And don't forget to turn the light,
With us up early every day
We like to have an early night."*

On Sunday Dad's the first to rise
And venture off along the prom
To chat to fishermen at times
And ask the stranger where he's from.

The paper shop's his port of call
And say hello to Mrs Green,
A change of wind, she gloomy tells,
Will surely bring a rainy scene.

At breakfast time we all arrive
At tables numbered one to ten
And make polite but oh-so-quiet
Conversation now and then.

The week begins to fall in place:
It's Tuesday boating, Wednesday shops,
And oh dear, Mrs Green was right,
By Thursday it's the rain that drops.

Although it pours we watch the sea,
The great big waves that blow the crafts,
And then explore the pleasure beach
To watch the clown who always laughs.

On Saturday we start to pack
A suitcase till the lid is bent
With all the clothes we never wore,
But brought in case of accident.

The old jalopy takes the load,
Yet with each package gives a moan,
It seems to know it's got the job
Of taking all the party home.

Mum checks and double-checks our room
To see we don't leave anything,
And even goes on hands and knees
As though she'd lost a diamond ring.

Our farewells done, we board the car,
Up to our knees in sandy pile,
Dad says he'll clean it first job back
And we all give a knowing smile.

And sometime later, perhaps a week,
We hurry to the chemist's store
To finger over photographs
But what a few! We thought we'd more.

There's Dad asleep laid out in state
And Mother's hat looks quite absurd,
And Jane up to her head in sand
And who took that? It's come out blurred

One winter's night in years to come
When outside all is cold and rain,
We'll hand the pictures round and laugh
And live this week all through again.

THE DIET

Cream cakes, buns and marzipan,
Tins of biscuits laced with jam,
All are thoughts I put behind
Now that slimming's on my mind.

I'll go without those coffee breaks
And starve until my stomach aches,
No more will I go on a spree
Of buttered pikelets for my tea.

To lose a pound to me seems odd,
Resorting to steamed plaice or cod,
And eating mountains of green leaves
Like cabbage, lettuce, kidney beans.

I want to lose that vital inch
So that my clothes no longer pinch,
To try and look more elegant
And turn the head of every gent.

Now bread is out, I'm sure of that,
And so is pork, and bacon fat,
And chips with fried egg. Deary me!
What am I going to have for tea?

Now weeks have passed, and would you know,
My pencil figure starts to show,
I'll buy myself a brand new dress
And see just who I can impress.

I meet some friends I haven't seen
For quite a while, it must have been.
What's that they say? I'm looking fit,
And what? I haven't changed a bit.

MY BATH

I put my right foot in with care,
The water's not too hot,
Now lower myself through soapy layer,
I'm in, and half an hour I've got.

I lay back, sinking to my neck
To contemplate the ceiling,
When from the depths down underneath
I get a painful feeling.

I grope around to find the cause
Of my distress and troubles,
Oh! here it is, my son has left
His boat beneath the bubbles.

Well now it's in I'll play with it
And push it back and to,
Now bomb it with the sponge, oh dash!
That's splashed right in my shoe.

Enough of silliness and games
I'll lay back down again,
And plan the garden out this year
And hope it doesn't rain.

I must do something with that lawn,
I'll get a bag of fibre,
Good Heavens, what's that on the light?
It's surely not a spider?

"Who's banging on the bathroom door?
It's steamed up. Is it you?"

I ought to decorate the place,
It really needs a clean,
These white tiles have been on so long
They're almost turning green.

Where was I? Yes, the garden lawn,
It really is a sin,
Last time our neighbours saw it
They said, "Get McAlpines in."

But then the kids have got to play,
I must be fair on them,
The trouble is they will bring round
That crowd from number ten.

This bubble bath is not much good,
That label shows a lot,
If that girl there had what I've here
She'd show all that she'd got.

Who's banging on the bathroom door?
It's steamed up. Is it you?
You what? You're in a hurry,
And you want to use the loo?

THREE AGES OF MAN

It is morning.
Through my window I can see
The world, forever calling me,
Her treasures dangle before me,
I must reach out and touch them.

It is midday.
Through my window I can see
Endless years, security,
A self-made man, I and me,
I will sit back and rest.

It is evening.
Through my window I can see
A world that has just passed me by,
It leaves me alone, and weary,
Too late, I could have done more.

I AM YOUR GOD

Seek not for me in lofty buildings
Or call my name in holy shrines,
Waste not your hours with ponderous phrases,
Nor wade through tomes for holy lines.

I do not rest in your traditions,
I do not side with you in fight,
You will not find me through the scholar,
I am the day, I am the night.

Give me no labels for your comfort,
I am not Protestant or Jew,
Nor Pentecostal, Quaker, Moslem,
Sikh or Communist or Drew.

I am not part of any doctrine,
Sackcloth and ashes are not mine,
Burnt images do not impress me,
Nor does the candle at the shrine.

Ask not for me in petty squabbles
Nor give me praise for battles won,
I am the morning, I am the evening,
The breaking dawn, the setting sun.

I do not fret for your salvation,
The born again, the sacred few,
Priorities are your creation,
My Kingdom does not have a queue.

I am not tamed by rules of conduct,
Of blueprints drawn by human plan,
Call out for me with one cry only,
That I am God and you are man.

A SERMON ON THE MINISTER

Age 20–30
This then the novice, young and bold,
Telling the oldest story told,
Enthusiasm lifts his voice
And bids us all, "Let us rejoice."

He's done his homework for this hour,
Proclaiming of the Lord's great power.
His hymns are brisk, and what is more,
The tunes we've never heard before.

But never mind, he'll pull us through,
A pulpit solo to the pew,
His smile a little too sincere,
Stuck on upon arriving here.

His prayers are trendy, "here and now",
No mention of a "thee" or "thou",
It's, "Hear us God, forgive our pride,
And put to right the wrongs outside."

His sermon, confident, sincere,
Some well-known clichés dotted here,
He's seen the path! He knows the way!
While all the world has gone astray.

Why he's been picked to see the light
He isn't sure, but knows he's right,
God's good to him and life's a dream
(There's not much meat, but lots of cream).

And as we leave to shake his hand
With conversation yet more bland,
He nervously retreats to go,
He doesn't really want to know.

Age 35–50
And now the man of middle age
Who feels his part is that of sage,
Of patting children on the head
And quoting quotes he wished he'd said.

The scholar, he whose time is spent
In finding out what Jesus meant,
And over years perfects the art
Of taking every word apart.

And in his search to find a key
He loses his identity,
Becoming just a pleasing face
Who'll drink your tea or say your grace.

His well-worn sermon often starts
With verses, and it has three parts,
And then, to justify his claim,
Repeats his first line once again.

There'll be no shocks, no revelation,
This man has found his true vocation,
We sit and hear contentedly
His twenty-minute homily.

And at its close, we shake the hand
Of one who'll always understand,
A kindly shepherd to his sheep,
Beloved within the castle keep.

Age 65–70
Now getting on, he's reached a phase
When clergy are put out to graze,
A hamlet with a tiny flock
Whose houses are of tudor mock.

He speaks at ladies' teas and quotes
Of many humorous anecdotes,
He wears half gold-rim reading glasses
While preaching now to upper classes.

His tales are pleasing fodder food
Which leave us feeling rather good,
Tradition is his constant note
And no one here will rock the boat.

Upon Death
And on his epitaph will read
The simple truth, "He served their need",
To each his own, he gave his best
With little help to aid his quest.

For some who knew him sought the truth,
While others simply wanted proof,
And he, poor soul, was probably
Just as confused as you and me.

SEARCHING

Why, when our spirits strive for peace,
Must war and suffering increase?
When will we give the still small voice?
A chance to say, there is a choice.
Our ego, mindless, pompous, hard,
Drives through its will with disregard,
And treads on carefully planted seeds,
Instead of flowers, we nurture weeds.
We harbour grudges for so long,
Righteously name them right and wrong,
We condemn morals right on cue,
Forgetting others' point of view,
And let off steam on this and that
Behind the guise of friendly chat.
We tear our neighbours into shreds
Because "She never makes her beds".
The very folk we frown upon
Become the rope they hang us on,
We prattle on with endless zest
On people's worst and not their best.
How simple it is to condemn
The failures of our fellow men,
We join so easily the crowd
That shouts for justice long and loud,
Deaf to the Master's voice alone,
He without sin may cast a stone.
Lord, may we pray and not forget
We are the sinners sinning yet,
It was for us you lived and died
For me that you were crucified.

BARRIERS

A crowd once arrived at the heavenly gate
And they grew ill at ease when they found they'd to wait.
"Let us in," each one cried, "Let us each state our case,
For we are God's chosen, He has saved us a place."

And while they were standing in fear and unrest,
They decided among them to first take a test,
That each should explain while he stood on his own
Why the gates should be opened for just him alone.

A C of E Bishop was first up to speak,
He said, "Look at my cassock, it's pressed every week,
And my crook has been brasso'd, see how it shines bright,
In my church we've stained windows that colour the light."

Then the Catholic cried out, "Very good, but see here,
For I have a Saint every month of the year,
And a plaster Madonna and incense galore,
And I place holy water inside my front door."

Then the Orthodox Jew said, "No, no, you are wrong,
You can see I am holy, my beads are so long,
I wear a black coat and I don a black hat,
Even you must agree, that there's merit in that."

Then the Methodist said, "I am not so austere,
But I don't hold with gambling or drinking of beer,
And on Sundays I don't lift a finger you see,
Well, perhaps I watch telly, so bully for me."

Then up rose a Mormon and said, "All my life
I have married a wife, and a wife, and a wife,
A tenth of my income I've given away,
And I've knocked on more doors than I really could say."

And then stood a Sikh, who proclaimed at some length
That not cutting one's hair was of spiritual strength,
But he was cried down by an old Buddhist monk
Who had shaved all his head and resembled a punk.

He said, "Baldness will bring you a spiritual bliss."
"Not so," cried the Guru, "It's sitting like this."
Then a Monk from a monastery, "silent in life",
Said, "I've sacrificed everything, even a wife."

Then a louder voice echoed from out of the crowd,
"Jehovah's my witness, I'll shout it out loud,
And I have every answer in chapter and verse
So I won't give my blood or I'll suffer God's curse."

And while they all argued their own case was right,
Their voices grew louder as day followed night,
And soon fists were waving and threats being said,
What they'd practised in life they'd continue though dead.

Then a child came along and the gates opened wide,
Then they closed with a bang as she entered inside,
"Why her?" came the voices from outside the wall,
"What has she done so special? She's really quite small."

"I will tell you quite simply," said he at the gate,
"The reason she entered while you have to wait.
No one told her of sin, so she lived her life through,
Free from doctrine and humbug that separate you.

"She claimed no allegiance to prophet or creed,
But humbly gave service to others in need,
She would listen to all, but was never deceived
That the Kingdom of Heaven was for just who believed."

"Is it not?" came the shouts from the crowd held outside,
"Have our teachings been false, are our statements denied?"
Then the man at the gate said, "You each drew your plan,
And you cluttered up God with the trappings of man.

"For you held to your doctrine from first to the last,
But your God was too small, for the mould you have cast
Was too pious and offered to only a few,
Yet God is creation, the universe through.

"He is not Father Christmas who has to be pleased,
Nor yet some great tyrant who must be appeased.
He is God! He is stone, He is fire, He is wood.
You can't win his approval through just being good.

"And there is no set pattern or test to achieve,
There is no right of entry for those who believe,
Come in one, come in all, you are part of His race,
You have lived in His world, you are in His embrace."

A CHRISTMAS GIFT

Come buy! Come buy! Shop windows cry,
Come save on special offers,
Don't hesitate, you'll be too late,
Come fill our bursting coffers.

With shelves piled high to catch the eye
Of every person passing,
A spending spree of Christmas glee
Each trader is amassing.

I stand among the bustling throng
And watch them hurry by me,
The glittering windows all around
Have Christmas gifts to ply me.

I look and sigh and wonder why
The shops have all the glory,
While the churches empty of their flock
Retell the Christmas story.

A tale of babe in manger laid
And shepherds fast asleep,
Of Angel song they brought along
A lamb to Jesu's feet.

The story then tells of three men
Whose wisdom was renown,
They sought a King their gifts to bring
And leave at Bethlehem town.

*"The glittering windows all around
Have Christmas gifts to ply me."*

A simple tale, and almost pale
Against today's accounts,
And yet the giving is the same
In large or small amounts.

That tale of fame applies the same
Today as years ago,
Shepherds and Kings gave precious things
Because they loved him so.

And surely we our friendship see
As something worth a price,
What better way to show our love
Than giving something nice.

There is a time to give too much,
A time to overspend,
That time is Christmas with a gift
That says, "I love you, friend."

JUST ANOTHER TALE?

Just two peering faces
In the evening gloom,
Trying to find places,
Searching for a room.

Just a worried husband
Concerned to go no more,
Finding in a strange land
No one at the door.

Just a friendly landlord
At the local inn,
Giving all he could afford:
A barn to shelter in.

Just a group of cattle
Watching in the night,
Hearing vessels rattle
Round a lantern light.

Just another labour,
No one close at hand,
Nothing in her favour
But a swaddling band.

Just a weary flock of sheep
There to see the scene,
First to hear the baby weep
In that stable mean.

Just another baby,
Another mouth to feed,
Born of mortal lady,
Yet of Godly seed.

Just a child and mother
Sheltering in a barn,
Just like any other,
Trying to keep warm.

Just a rough-hewn manger
Where the baby laid,
A refugee, a stranger,
Was the price he paid.

Just another story?
No: that babe is King,
And of his power and glory
May we forever sing.

NATIVITY (Yorkshire Dialect)

I'll tell you a tale of a couple,
Young lovers they were, I've no doubt,
And they'd come up to Bethlehem city,
Young Joseph and Mary, his spouse.

Now Mary were having a baby,
It were due to arrive any day,
So Joseph looked round for a lodging,
A boarding house where they could stay.

The town were so crowded with people
And he walked for an hour or more,
"Full up" were the answer they gave him
As he knocked on most every door.

He came to a pub on a corner,
It weren't what he first had in mind,
But by now he was getting quite desperate
And the landlord looked thoughtful and kind.

"Can you fix us up with a room mate?"
Joseph said with despair in his face,
"I'm sorry I can't," said the landlord,
"I've not a square inch in the place."

Joseph turned and was just about leaving,
His hand were on't sneck of the door,
When landlord said, "Eh, I've a stable,
If you want to kip down on the floor."

Joseph thought for a while about Mary,
She was all in with the journey that day,
So he said to the landlord, "I'll take it,
We'll be out of the cold anyway."

When they got into't stable they sat down
On a bundle of hay in the stall,
Joseph sighed, but Mary said wryly,
"It's better than nothing at all."

The baby were born early morning
By the light of a paraffin lamp,
And they wrapped it in swaddling blankets
In that stable so cold and so damp.

"Let's put him in't manger," said Joseph,
It'll 'appen serve as a cot."
And the animals looked in amazement
When they saw what a stranger they'd got.

In a field just outside of the city
Shepherds guarded their sheep overnight,
When suddenly out of the black sky
Came a vision that gave 'em a fright.

It were angels, they'd come with a message,
It were good news, so Gabriel said,
He told them to look in a stable
To find baby in't manger bed.

With excitement they set off for't city,
Though weary, they most of them ran,
As they knew that this babe were important
They took him a gift of a lamb.

When they got to the stable they looked in
And saw the young couple with lad,
Joseph said, "Come in and you're welcome."
And their faces were cheerful and glad.

They gave little lad what they'd brought him:
A baby lamb set down on't floor,
And rejoicing they set off for t'country
And guarding their sheep as before.

At this time of year the same message
Is brought to us over the years,
Though we don't see no radiant angels
Or hear heavenly choirs in our ears.

Let's turn from our jobs like them shepherds
And rejoice like they did, that first morn,
Let us carry our gifts to that baby
And give thanks for that child that is born.

EE! WOT A CHRISTMAS! (Yorkshire Dialect)

One day while Mary were sewing
This Angel appeared and he spoke,
He said, "Mary, you're having a baby,
Although you're not wed to a bloke.

"But don't let this happening alarm you
'Cause I bring you this message from t'Head,
And he's chosen your name out of thousands."
"You've got to be joking," she said,

"I'm nowt but a lass with no money,
And I'm sure I don't mix with right set,
And while I've a liking for Joseph,
I weren't thinking of marrying yet."

"Come, come now," said Gabriel kindly,
"I thought I were bringing good news."
"Well that's all very well," answered Mary,
"But you might have considered my views."

"Me and Joseph have just got acquainted,
And I'm dreading to think what he'll say,
But I don't think he'll be very happy
When I tell him I'm in't family way."

Then Mary said, "You've brought the message
Like a thunderbolt out of the blue,
So while you're down here playing postman
You can go round and tell Joseph too."

" 'Me and Joseph have just got acquainted,
And I'm dreading to think what he'll say.' "

"Nay," said Gabriel, looking downhearted,
"I'm top man in heaven where I'm from,
And I only come down for Messiahs
I'm not here to pass messages on."

"Now be fair," answered Mary, "And listen,
If I'm having this baby you say,
The least you can do is tell him,
'Cause I'll never explain it away."

"Very well, you've convinced me," said Angel,
"I'll pop round with a word in his ear."
"While you're at it," said Mary, "Tell neighbours,
They'll be gossiping now till next year."

Well, after the first weeks of turmoil
Everything settled down as before,
And nine months went by without trouble
Till a letter arrived through the door.

"Who's it from?" Mary thought, looking puzzled,
While she opened it up with great care,
"Jerusalem's place it were posted,
But who do we know who lives there?"

It were quite an official announcement
Wrote in phrases she couldn't understand,
But the gist of the message were simple,
It were certainly not what they'd planned.

It read, "We are having a census,
And to make sure we've got figures right
Will you please make a personal appearance
With your passport on Saturday night."

"Thank goodness," said Joseph, now smiling,
As he sank down in't chair to relax,
"When I saw that buff envelope coming
I thought they were wanting more tax."

"There's a snag," Mary said, looking dismal,
"You might not have taxman to pay,
But Bethlehem city's where't poll is,
And by gum, that's an awful long way."

"You're right, Bethlehem's quite a journey
With you in that state," Joseph said,
"And you're going to be riding a donkey
When really you should be in bed."

When they got into Bethlehem city
Mary said, "Where we going to stay?"
"Well I haven't a clue," Joseph answered,
"But I'll give it some thought during day."

Mary weren't very pleased with his answer
For baby were starting to call,
She were weary with overland journey,
And donkey were flagging an' all.

"I'm looking for rooms," Joseph shouted,
And an innkeeper said, "Aren't we all!"
"But I've just got a room in the annexe,
We've done it all out like a stall."

Mary said, when she looked in at stable,
"Is this really the best you can do?
I'd much rather have stayed at the Hilton,
It's last time I leave bookings to you."

Well both blamed each other for't mishap
And neither would give or concede,
Then Mary shouts, "Baby's arriving!"
And Joseph said, "That's all we need."

"Don't just stand there," said Mary, "Get water,
See landlord or go and enquire."
"It's baby you're having," said Joseph,
"You're not going to put out a fire!"

Well, after a little explaining
Joseph went round to landlord to say,
Could he have some hot water, and landlord replied
That he'd put kettle on right away.

Well, baby were born early morning
And they laid little lad in some straw,
And when news of the birth got to landlord,
All't neighbours came in from next door.

Well, news travelled fast in that country:
Soon all't city knew what had occurred,
In fact Gabriel went to tell shepherds
And they said that they'd already heard.

But no matter, they'd go and see't baby,
Gabriel said, "Aren't you going to get changed?"
"What, at this time of night?" replied shepherds,
"You should have these things better arranged."

"Let's take baby a gift," said a shepherd,
"Like a pair of new shoes or a cap."
But at finish they took him a new lamb,
Though it proved very awkward to wrap.

Then they went into t'stable to see him
And they found little lad in a stall,
And Joseph were all but for chucking 'em out
When one of them said, "I'n't he small?"

Then one said, "Don't leave him in there love,
'Cause in't morning when animals wake,
There's such a poor light in this stable
They might eat little lad by mistake."

Some time later three kings paid a visit,
On their fingers they wore diamond rings,
But when they announced what their names were
Joseph said that he'd just call them "kings".

They said, "We've brought gifts for the kiddie,
There's frankincense, gold and there's myrrh."
Joseph wished they'd have bought him a train set
Or a nice box of chocolates for her.

But no matter, at least they'd bought summat,
It were quality goods and not trash,
Joseph said that he'd go round to't pawn shop
And see if he could change them for cash.

By the way, I think I should tell you
That this story of which I now speak,
It all happened some two thousand years since —
Or will it all happen next week?

THE SPIRIT OF CHRISTMAS

I looked for Christ this Christmas,
But was told it would be hard
To see Him in the modern man,
For Christ there's no regard.
But I found Him.

You'll never see Him these days,
I was told with great dismay,
They're all commercial trappings
That are out upon display.
But I found Him.

There are toys for endless children,
Gifts and presents by the score,
You won't find Christ in that lot:
He's been squeezed out of the door.
But I found Him.

The King of Christmas nowadays
Is not the one you seek,
The only God is money
And the pay night once a week.
But I found Him.

I'll tell you where I found Him,
He's not really hard to find,
It's just that folk are busy
While others are too blind.
Yes, I found Him.

I saw Him in an eager face
Pressed up against the glass
Of a little toy shop window
And she did not see me pass.
There was happiness.

I saw Him in a mother's care:
She bought her child a bike,
While her shabby coat would have to do
Although it looked a sight.
There was sacrifice.

I saw Him in a bus queue
As a gang of youths made way
To let a blind man get on first,
"Come on," I heard them say.
There was care.

I saw a council, hard as nails,
And working very slow
Push through a plan for Christmas lights
To make a cheerful show.
There was heart.

I saw a miser buy a gift,
And though the gift was small,
If it hadn't been for Christmas
There would have been no gift at all.
There was kindness.

I saw young love go hand in hand
Along a crowded street,
Their faces lit with happiness,
The world for them complete.
There was love.

I saw the people go to church
With hearts so full with joy
To sing their glad hosannas
To praise the new-born boy.
There was joy.

For though these people knew not,
I could one moment see,
He said, "To do it unto others, so
You do it unto me."
There was Christ.

For love and joy and happiness
Are all we can afford
At the blessed time of Christmas
When we worship Christ the Lord.
Let us adore Him.

CHRISTMAS CARDS

There's Mary, John and family,
There's Ruth and Mrs Stocks,
There's cousin Fred, oh no, he's dead,
And I've gone and bought him socks.

There's Julie, Jack and Freda,
Aunt Maud, she's such a dear.
On second thoughts I'll leave her out,
She missed me off last year.

I must send one to Alice,
I've not seen her for a while,
And it must be all of twenty years
Since last I saw her smile.

And then there's Margaret's family,
Her husband Tom takes snuff,
I'll not send one with rabbits on,
Their family's big enough.

There's Ethel, Ron and Marjorie,
Mrs Gore at number ten,
Who stares behind her curtains
At the sight of any men.

Next door will have to have one,
Though in fact I seldom see her,
I'd sooner wish her far enough
Than greetings of the year.

I'd best send this religious card
To Caroline and Joe,
Of all the Christian people
They're the only ones I know.

And then there's Harry Butterfield
At local butcher's shop,
I'll keep the proper side of him
And get an extra chop.

How many's that? It must be twelve,
I'll suffer writer's cramp,
And now I come to think of it
I can't afford a stamp.

"On second thoughts I'll leave her out,
She missed me off last year."

They say there is enough for all,
If everyone who could
Would send some of their plenty
And so share the global food.

But wouldn't it be simpler
To allow a shower or two?
So the whole world could live decently,
And not the lucky few.

So, Father, in your wisdom,
Don't condemn me out of hand,
I'm just one of many millions
Who will never understand.

NEW YEAR

Come, herald of this bright new year,
Gay messenger all hailed in song,
Yet will your promises betray
The hope that is awaited long?

What tune of merriment sung now
Will last into a second verse?
What harmonies or surging tones
Will end discordinate, or worse?

Your long-awaited spirit soars
Throughout the land in hearts of men,
And ashes from the fires long dead
Are kindled to a flame again.

Timbers of hope and coals of peace
Are heaped upon the bright façade,
With each a wish against all hope
That truth will overcome charade.

Wishes and longings, hopes and fears
Are thrown before thy wingèd form,
And prayers are offered to the gods
For a safe and painless passage home.

Thus we are made of hope and fear
To long for happiness supreme,
We are but foolish miscreants
Who steer a course to seek a dream.

Come, herald of the bright new year,
Let trumpets sound and anthems soar,
We'll raise a glass to Auld Lang Syne
And promises oft made before.

POETRY LESSON 1

I've heard in my time lots of poetry,
So I think maybe I'll have a go,
After all its really quite easy
Once the words get into a rhythm.

I think that I'll write about roses,
A beautiful delicate flower,
Their scent and colours delightful,
And I look at them many a day.

Their blooms come in all shapes and sizes,
Some are open and some in tight bud,
I've only a very small garden
But I'd grow dozens more if I had room.

I just love to sit among flowers
And soak up the beautiful view,
On some sunny day if you visit
You can sit in my garden as well.

I think I could take to this poetry,
I quite enjoyed writing this verse,
And let's face it, I may not be Wordsworth,
But in my my time I've heard a lot not as good.

"I think I could take to this poetry,
I quite enjoyed writing this verse."

LEAP YEAR

I'm a modest man, I must tell you,
But people that know me will swear
That when I was quite a bit younger
I had quite a good head of hair.

My physique was a sight to amaze you,
I had biceps as big as your fists,
I dressed like a gent up from London
And wore perfume called "Love in a Mist".

You can gather from this that the ladies
Would very near faint as I passed,
They would swoon and come over all silly
If I spoke to an odd one at last.

My days were just one long engagement
With society's cream of the town,
If I took a young thing to the pictures
We'd sit in best seats (half a crown).

On Saturday nights I'd go dancing
To "Locarno" or p'raps City Hall,
And it weren't very long into't evening
When I'd dance with the belle of the ball.

The girls would just throw themselves at me,
After all I were really a catch,
Clark Gable were fine at the pictures
But with me he were never a match.

I'd dance for the whole of the evening
With Hazel or Rita or Pam,
Then I'd wave goodbye with a kiss and a sigh
And then go back home on the tram.

Of course all of this had to finish
When I first met my present sweetheart,
Jean was different from all of the others:
She were bigger than me for a start.

She bullied me into a wedding,
It happened in such a short time,
I could have had girls by the dozen,
But she stopped me while still in my prime.

After twenty-nine years I'm still with her,
She just loves looking after me so,
With her washing and ironing and cleaning
Well I haven't the heart just to go.

When I heard that this year were a leap year
My excitement I couldn't restrain,
If I went on the town like the old days
Girls would chuck themselves at me again.

But at first I thought, "best try the water
Before I up sticks and walk out,"
But with good looks like mine in a leap year
I'd very soon click, there's no doubt.

I decided to go to a disco
In order to turn on my charm,
But I got some strange looks from the doorman
Who had a tattoo on his arm.

He said, "Oi mush, just where are you going?
Dressed up in that blue suit and tie.
We had fancy dress here last Tuesday."
Then he gave me a poke in the eye.

At the pay desk I put down a pound coin
And said, "Keep the change" with a grin.
But the chap said, "You'd better put four more down,
That is if you want to get in."

Well I paid and went into this dark room
Where a band made a terrible row,
Never mind, I thought, once it has tuned up
It could play a waltz anytime now.

The floor was just full of gyration,
So I thought I'd join in with the crowd,
I walked up to a girl in the corner
Who had pink hair and wore a white shroud.

"Good evening," I said in me best voice,
"Would you care to join me on the floor?"
She said, "No thank you Grandad, I'm smoking,
But try her over there by the door."

She pointed across to a corner
Where this youngster sat drinking a coke,
She wore jeans and a mohican haircut,
In truth she looked more like a bloke.

I said, "Hi baby, how about grooving?
Let you and me make the night roar."
"By the age of you love," she said tersely,
"You'll be lucky if you make the floor."

By now I was feeling quite tired,
Well it must have been quarter to nine,
At home I'd have cocoa and biscuits,
But all they sold here was stale wine.

So I left and got into a taxi,
I said, "Take me to where it's all at."
So he drove me to just round the corner
To a place that was called the "Black Cat".

There was this girl stood inside the doorway,
I said, "Excuse me, I'd like to pass through."
She said, "Really I should see your ticket,
But your bus pass will probably do."

I ignored her sarcastic comment
And proceeded to enter the hall,
Then another girl showed me a table
That was jammed up against a brick wall.

I'd only been sat there a minute
When this lady came over to me,
She said, "What can I do to amuse you?"
So I said, "Could you get me a tea?"

She just laughed and threw both her arms round me
And said, "Wouldn't you like to play games?"
I said, "Yes, but I've not brought me dart board,
And it's too dark to play snooker frames."

The next thing I heard was a whistle
And police seen to come through the floor,
I was handcuffed to one in a jiffy
Who marched me non-stop through the door.

My case came up following morning,
So I told them about my mishap,
How I'd wanted just one night of romance,
But had fallen right into a trap.

The judge gave his learned opinion
And said, "This is a terrible thing."
Then he leaned over't bench and said softly,
"Here's me phone, next time give me a ring."

I'm back at home now with the missus,
It all went wrong somewhere, somehow,
My leap year romance was a pipe dream,
But just wait until four years from now.

A WINTER'S NIGHT ON THE FARM

Softly the midnight sky
Holding her stars aloft
Fills every field and hedge,
Shadows each barn and croft.

Frosty the grassy tufts,
Needles now tempered white,
Tableau an icy pose,
Reaching the silver night.

Howling the winter chill
Rounding the gated yard
Blowing a blustery tune
Over each black facade.

On into open moors,
Low now the humming tone,
Lifeless the bracken leaf,
Cold is the granite stone.

Warm on the stable floor
Cows sleep amid the hay,
Silent and motionless
Steaming their breath away.

Dog on the kitchen rug,
Lulled by the ticking clock,
Large as a fist the key
Turned in the frozen lock.

Fire embers in the hearth
Send out an amber glow,
Outside the winter's chill
Scatters the falling snow.

Snug in the upper room
Farmer and farmer's wife
Sleep under eiderdown
Safe from the harms of life.

NOT NOW
(A Thought of Dying)

Winter

Not now, while frosted grass
On pale white fields reflect the hazy sun,
And 'neath a frozen blanket cold
New life has yet begun.

While crack and crackle freezing barks
Echo down empty lanes,
And squirrels forage in the earth
To gain the frozen grains.

Though bleak this landscape winter white,
It offers grandeur of delight.

Spring

Not now, while warmer winds excite the trees
And stir the shady dell,
While daffodils turn up their heads to
Herald the bluebell.

While tractors furrow patchwork fields
With clouds of hungry birds,
And sheep and cow mow shades of green
Lethargically in herds.

To look upon this pastoral sea
Is food and drink and life to me.

Summer

Not now, while corn is on the stem
And dappled trees give shade,
When parks are filled with children
Fishing with nets they've made.

When everything that lives in nature blossoms
And bees are busy buzzing on the wing,
When all the earth surrenders up its portion
And in the heated stillness, crickets sing.

Not now, while nature's perfumes stir my senses,
Or while such sights of glory fill my eyes,
While meadow lands unfold lush green before me,
A blessèd realm under these English skies.

Though this may be a transient scene,
It offers me a peace serene.

Autumn

Not now, while fulsome trees are lying heavy
And ripening berries bunch in ruby red,
When bronze and ochre leaves give up their perches
To flutter down into a golden bed.

When barns are full of summer's ripening harvest
And farmers take a break from year-long toil,
When fires are set along the lines of stubble
And once again the plough returns the soil.

These rolling seasons lift my heart,
O Lord, I cannot now depart.

JUMBLE

I've just been to a jumble sale market
Round the corner at Cuthbert's Church Hall,
The bargains I've got would amaze you
And they're all from the bric-a-brac stall.

You see this? Well it cost me ten shillings,
Or in modern day terms, fifty pence,
It's a thing you open a tin with,
Or free a cow stuck on a fence.

Then there's this chiming clock — isn't it lovely?
Once I've cleaned off the grease and the grime,
I'll get some new works and some fingers,
Then I bet it will keep perfect time.

Lady Morbrough brought this from the Manor,
They say it was hung on the stairs,
I don't really think I can use it,
But I got it because it was hers.

Now just look at this shoe — it's real leather,
The price of these new is a crime,
It's a pity I've just got the one though,
But I might get the other next time.

What about this Ming vase, made in China?
Look, there's dragons all over the place,
I know it's all crazy, but look underneath,
It says "Made in Hong Kong" on the base.

I managed to get this nice jumper,
Well I've always liked things done in blue,
It's a shame that there's only one sleeve left,
But Mrs Drake wanted it too.

These pot ducks will look lovely on my wall,
They'll remind me of days by the sea,
There's one with the wings that are broken,
But I'll nail that behind the settee.

Mind you, I've been done with these teaspoons,
I've found they're not silver at all,
When I've cleaned them I've noticed they're EPNS,
And I forked 20p out an' all.

Still it's all in a good cause they tell me,
They're raising the funds for the spire,
And the vicar said my contribution
Will build it another inch higher.

I'n't funny how somebody's rubbish
Is often a treasure to me,
I suppose I'm not worth much to others
But in God's hands, I hope I might be.

FOOTBALL CRAZY

That referee ought to be locked up,
It were never in this world a free kick,
And what is he waving his arms for?
He'd do better to wave a white stick.

He should have been pensioned off years since,
He's ninety-five if he's a day,
He's not seen that ball since they started,
And we're nearly an hour into play.

Of course this team's known for its fouling,
Well they cheat if you want to be blunt,
They went three games with no score against them
'Cause their goal nets were on back to front.

And him on't left wing's a right baby,
If they nudge him he thinks it's a crime,
No wonder they nicknamed him "lino",
He's been on't floor that many times.

It's time they spent money on players,
But this management don't know a thing,
They heard Arthur Scargill's a striker
So they bought him to play on't right wing.

Bill Tanner's been with them three seasons
And they always play him centre-half,
If it comes on to rain or turns windy
He plays in his coat, hat and scarf.

And that goalie's a seven-stone weakling,
His face is as white as a ghost,
When he stands to one side of the goalmouth
You just can't tell which is the post.

And look at Phil Curtiss at full-back,
I've not seen him move this last hour,
For what use he is to the others
He might just as well stay in the shower.

Hello, Jack's got a boot into that one,
It's a pity it wasn't the ball,
It's their number 10, look he's writhing,
He must have tripped over to fall.

Just look at Bill Wiggins, he's useless,
There's more brains in a bucket of sand,
When they told him last week to play sweeper
He came out with a brush in his hand.

Now then, Harris has moved into their half,
Mind, I've said all along he's no good,
He's tackled a man, now he's past him,
Now he's scored! Well, I knew that he would.

Is that whistle they're blowing for half-time?
Well I'd better get back to my post,
When they're feeling dejected and weary
That's the time they need manager most!

JEAN

My missus is one in a million,
She's a wonder at making ends meet,
She can take out a pound
And make it go round
Till it feeds everyone in the street.

But just let her loose in a clothes shop
And something inside her just snaps,
If she sees the word "Sale"
She can clear a dress rail
Like a dog coming out of the traps.

Her baking just has to be tasted,
Her sponges are light as a dream,
She can do a soufflé
Any hour of the day
And her custards are smoother than cream.

But mention the magic word "fashion"
And she changes from Jekyll to Hyde,
Let her wander through "Modes"
And her money erodes
And all reason is thrown to one side.

She reads books that would really amaze you,
Her knowledge I'll never achieve,
She can quote Voltaire
Or recite Rupert Bear
And she's read "War and Peace" I believe.

But just let her walk in a shoe shop,
You can hear the assistants all groan,
Then out of despair
She'll buy a new pair
That just look the same as her own.

At parties there's nobody like her,
She will mix with the highest or low,
She will circulate round
Making comments profound
And keep smiling until they all go.

But take her to some shopping precinct,
She can sniff out a dress shop for miles,
She's got some kind of nose
For dresses or hose
Or shoe shops with fifty-odd styles.

She's a voice like an angel from heaven,
She can charm the birds out of the skies,
With a melody fair
She can sing you an air
That will quickly bring tears to your eyes.

But just give her house-keeping money
To go out and buy stuff like bread,
She'll come back with things
Like a scarf and ear-rings
Or a new coat and handbag instead.

At Jaeger she knows every item,
She can tell you the price at a glance,
She's been in such a lot
That last Tuesday she got
An invite to the Annual Dance.

Just to walk in our house would amaze you,
There are clothes of all sorts down the hall,
There are crepes and velours
Which extend to all floors
And dresses that stretch wall to wall.

She always asks my opinion,
Like, shall she choose yellow or red,
Then when I've had my say
She'll take it away
And then buy the green one instead.

I vowed on the day we were married
That I'd take her for better or worse,
But nobody said
On the day I were wed
That she suffered from bottomless purse.

Now don't get me wrong, it's not her fault,
As a child she weren't properly brought up
So when things get bad
And she's desperate or sad
She rings "Clothes Anonymous" up.

If it weren't for her beauty I'd leave her,
If it weren't for her voice I'd just go,
But to see her so fair
With her lovely red hair
I'm afraid that I just can't say no.

So I'll just have to part with my money
In order to keep wedded bliss,
She'll continue to shine
In clothes that look fine
While I dress up from Oxfam, like this.

I MIGHT HAVE BEEN

Some people are born to be famous
While others among us make do
With just being nobody special,
We live and we just muddle through.

So I cast me mind back through the ages
To ponder on who I might be,
Someone gallant and brave and good looking
Instead of just being plain me.

Now Hadrian, he became famous
'Cause he got job of building a wall,
But he'd scarce got last brick in position
When they said it weren't needed at all.

He explained to the King down in London
That he'd made Britain into two lands,
And he'd worn out five hods in the process
And cement had played hell with his hands.

But King would have none of his protest
And paid him no more than a crown,
So feeling annoyed at the pittance
He went back and pulled it all down.

He said that his talent was wasted
And the money he got was unfair,
So he took the first boat out to China
For he heard they'd a job going there.

And then there's that fellow called Nelson,
He went out and won us a war,
But at finish he'd lost both an arm and an eye
Or he said that he would have done more.

He gave up all hopes of promotion
Which left him quite low and bereft,
But he said, "If I keep on at this rate,
In ten years I'll have nothing left."

I quite fancy that Boadicea,
They say she had wonderful eyes,
She also had blades sticking out of her cart
So her subjects were cut down to size.

Now what about me being Monty,
In the annals of war he stands tall,
I quite fancy leading an army of men
But berets don't suit me at all.

I wouldn't mind being a painter
And do works of art like Van Gogh,
But I wouldn't see what's on my canvas
'Cause my glasses would keep falling off.

I think that I could have been Shakespeare,
Writing plays and attending first nights,
But I'm not very keen on his dress sense
And my legs would look silly in tights.

Then of course I could sing like Caruso
And perform in the great Albert Hall,
Or again I could be a pop singer
And for that I'd need no voice at all.

But looking back over these heroes,
They all died in a bit of jam,
And let's face it, they all had their Achilles heel,
While I'm perfect the way that I am.

HANDYMAN

Wife Don't just sit there and look at the telly,
     You should have something better to do,
     There's some holes in the stairs and a dozen
       repairs,
     Surely you must have noticed them too?

Husband Yes I know love, but look at it this way,
     This programme is on D.I.Y.,
     I'll just watch it another ten minutes
     Then I'll give built-in wardrobes a try.

Wife Are you glued to that chair for the evening?
     You promised you'd see to that door,
     I've only to cough and the handle falls off
     And I can't turn the key anymore.

Husband I'll start it first thing in the morning,
     You can't rush these things right away,
     I'll just see the news, 'cause it widens my
      views,
     And when that's done it's Match of the Day.

Wife Have you seen that damp patch in our
      bedroom?
     That ceiling's a terrible sight,
     If you don't get a slater, then sooner or later
     We'll see the stars come out at night.

"I'll just watch Black Adder and then get a ladder,
Or I'll do it when Wogan is through."

Husband   Now don't go exciting yourself love,
               It won't take a minute to do,
               I'll just watch Black Adder and then get a
                    ladder,
               Or I'll do it when Wogan is through.

Wife   It's a wonder your legs haven't rooted,
               You've sat there so long in that chair,
               While I'm hours at the sink
               You just sit there and think
               Or your eyes just glaze over and stare.

Husband   To do a job right it needs planning,
              If they're done wrong you'll end up in tears,
              You'll find all the best men
              Start with paper and pen
              And watch Blankety Blank for ideas.

Wife   Are you moving, or shall I vac round you?
              Have you seen that green mark on the wall?
              It goes down to the floor
              And the woman next door
              Says it comes through on her side an' all.

Husband   I've told you I'll see to it sometime,
              Goodness me it'll not take me long,
              I'll just see this drama, then watch
                  Panorama,
              Oh, and then it's The Road to Hong Kong.

Wife   My mother was right, you're just useless,
              Can't you see the house falling apart?
              From cellar to ceiling the paintwork is
                  peeling,
              At least you could get up and start.

Husband   You're right love, I will make the effort,
              There's no time like the present they say,
              But if I make a mess
              It might cause you distress
              So I'll leave it till some other day.

100

NEIGHBOURS

"Eh up," she said, leaning on't fencing
Which nearly gave way 'neath her weight,
"Have you heard what they're saying on't corner
About him what goes in number eight?

"Mrs Kirk, who knows everyone's business,
Said he's tallyman paying a call,
But her at fourteen says she's met him
And he doesn't collect owt at all.

"Mrs King does her steps on a Friday
And can see her front door when he knocks,
But I don't like to ask her for details
'Cause she has to stand up on two blocks.

"He's nobody I've seen in't High Street
So I don't think he owns any shops,
Though Mrs Green swears he's a butcher
And says he once served her with chops.

"Well, I'm not one to go spreading gossip,
I've got too much to do with me time,
But old Mrs Lunt down at twenty
Says he took in a big bag of lime.

"Well her garden's the size of a blanket,
So what does she want with all that?
If you ask me, there's something amiss there
'Cause her husband's like twelve stone of fat.

"And of course he's been ill for a long time,
Well I've not seen him out on the street,
Mrs King saw her pawning his best shoes,
Goodness knows what she's done with his feet.

"You probably know we're not speaking,
Well we haven't since me and her crossed,
I just mentioned her windows were mucky
And she told me to go and get lost.

"You don't mean to tell me you know him!
And you say he's been sent from church hall?
He's the curate who's visiting sick folk?
Well . . . that's just what I thought an' all!"

SCOTLAND '88

We've just been away up to Scotland
And we stayed there just over a week,
Well, I don't want to put you off going
But they haven't a clue how to speak.

Their customs would really amaze you,
They have parties called "Ceilidhs" at night,
It's sort of a dance with a difference,
By nine o'clock everyone's tight.

They wear funny clothes, have you noticed?
The fellows look daft to be blunt,
They wear blouses and skirts like a woman
With handbags that hang down their front.

Then there's the language that's different:
I met one and said, "How d'yer do?"
Well, he fair shook me hand off its elbow,
Then he answered and said, "Hoots the noo!"

And the things that they give you for breakfast:
It was porridge, but made like cement,
It sat there and set in a big lump,
When I stuck in a spoon — it just bent.

They also eat stuff they call "haggis",
I don't just know where they get that,
But I pictured it when it had legs on
And it looked about size of a cat.

Their musical taste would amaze you,
It sounds like they've sat on a cat,
They get it by blowing an octopus up,
Well, you can't play a good tune like that.

At Oban, the place was deserted,
The whole town had taken to bed,
So I asked a policeman the reason,
"It's an annual flag day," he said.

For remembering names they're just hopeless,
I wouldn't give them nowt out of ten,
I kept saying, "I'm Terry from Sheffield,"
But they answered with, "Ay do yer Ken."

There were these fellows up in the Highlands,
They were chucking this telegraph pole,
When it kept falling over — I told them,
"It won't stand without digging a hole."

On our last night, we went Highland flinging
And we danced over swords on the floor,
But I tried it and cut both my toes off
So I'm not going back anymore.

A PRAYER OF THE HEART

Of all the living beauty
I may see in my last hour,
O Lord, I would be privileged
To look upon a flower.

What joy and gaiety divine
Encompassed in a span of thine,
A multicoloured song of bliss,
Lord, grant that I may look on this.

SUNDAY MORNING

Oh, the joy of Sunday solace,
Waking with the morning sun,
Rising just a little early
So to get the day begun.

Down to breakfast (toast and cornflakes),
Switching on the radio,
Tea and news are shared with planning
How the Sunday day will go.

First a walk up to St Andrews,
Striking at the quarter hour,
Hearing birds up in the tree tops,
Beauty to outshine the tower.

Slow the pace, reflect the moment,
Appreciate the here and now,
Drink in all of nature's bounty,
Dandelion and blossomed bough.

Home again, the working household
Breaks the stillness of the morn,
But I've had my morning worship
Alone with birds and trees and dawn.

MY CHURCH

They have no wings
These walls divine,
They sing of hymns
That are not mine.

And through these windows
Comes a light
That offers darkness
Such as night.

This pulpit where
Strong words abound
Leave me as though
On sinking ground.

Nothing of nature
Here is seen,
Except one spray
Of natural green.

One blush of colour
'Gainst a sea
Of polished painted property

This is not mine
This empty shell,
This hallowed place
I know so well.

Sooner my altar
Be a stone,
Weathered by wind
And rain alone.

With cloth of green
Where mosses grow,
A place that birds
And beasts shall know.

My gift to offer
But a flower,
Fresh as the moment
Of that hour.

So shall my song
Be with the birds,
The noisy sheep
And lowing herds.

The howling storm
The river's trill,
The silence of
An earth stood still.

And there my soul
Shall be outpoured,
For I shall see
Thy face, Lord.

THE MOUNTAIN
(On Seeing Ben Nevis)

Great was the hand that formed thy frame,
Cleaving thy fearful symmetry,
Mighty the scale of rock and ash
Now moulded into company.

Fateful the hour thy cauldron soared,
Blackening the very light of day,
Bruising the bare and barren land,
Melting the solid stone to clay.

Deafening the sound that roared and rang,
Blasting the empty space of time,
Sculpting the land with flame and fire,
Carving the mountain and the mine.

Jewelled now thy crown of frozen snow,
Greener the garlands of thy slopes,
Noble a statement of thy past,
Beacon to all man's future hopes.

SANTA'S LAMENT

I'm dreading it coming
But what can you do?
It's as timeless as dying
And hits you like 'flu.

It was all right to start with,
Well, more of lark,
I dressed up as Santa
And walked round in the dark.

Some children, God bless 'em,
Would put out a shoe,
And I'd pop in some sweets
Or a copper or two.

Well within a short time
Other kids got to hear,
And more shoes appeared
As each year followed year.

Word spread from my village
And travelled to town,
So that by the third Christmas
I never sat down.

And each year bigger shoes
Were put out on the door,
So that those with big feet
Would get goodies galore.

I got no direct thanks,
But the cobblers had views,
They said they were doing
A bomb in large shoes.

One Christmas it happened
Just as I had feared,
Outside of one door
A long stocking appeared.

Well now, don't get me wrong
I'm not some kind of prude,
But to put things in stockings
I feel rather rude.

Of course the idea caught on
And before you could sneeze
There were stockings galore
Just as bold as you please.

It gave me ideas
As I got to each door,
For I wondered who'd been
In that leg night before.

Some stockings were woolly
And milled up and small,
But some were them fishnets
With seams up and all.

I fair lost control
Just to see them hung there,
And if the house contained sisters
They put out a pair.

Something had to be done
Or I'd never get round,
I was too busy dreaming
To cover the ground.

Well, I needn't have worried
Or had any doubt,
For some greedy kid
Put a pillowcase out.

As before others followed
What one had begun,
So I got round much quicker
But not with such fun.

It was soon after that
That I got my first note,
It read, "Santa please send me
Some boots and a coat."

With no mention of toys
I thought, this is a fix,
For the coat size were 12
And the boot's size were 6.

From then on it snowballed
With letters galore,
I'd get up in a morning
And couldn't find my door.

I was working all hours
Which is not what I'd planned,
Then some elves said
"We'll come round and give you a hand."

Their foreman was Kevin
And small as a mouse,
Well, he needed a ladder
To paint a doll's house.

Then a jack-in-the-box
Was next thing they did,
Although it took six
Just to close down the lid.

By the end of the day
I must say they'd worked well,
And they'd turned out two scooters,
Four kites and a bell.

Well, with all this assistance
Production just soared,
So I acted as foreman
Until I got bored.

It were just before Christmas,
I saw what we'd got,
And I knew there was no way
I could carry that lot.

There were bicycles, tricycles,
Scooters and games,
There were pastry sets, prams,
Tins of paint and some trains.

There were books on discovery,
Books on new toys,
And some books I thought
Were too old for young boys.

There were "Ruperts" and "Beanos",
There was "Play Hour" and "Mirth",
And a book called "Oor Wullie"
For a lad up in Perth.

When I saw this great pile
I just murmured, "Oh dear,
To get that lot delivered
Will take me all year."

Then one of my elves said,
"It's transport you need,
Something quick like a sledge
That can travel at speed."

With no further ado
He knocked up a good sleigh,
"There you are now," he said,
"You'll get round in a day."

As we both looked with pride
At the sledge on the floor,
I thought of a snag
We'd not noticed before.

You see sledges are fine
If you visit a glen,
The trouble begins
When you come out again.

They won't go at all
If you're facing uphill,
And on level ground
They're inclined to stand still.

"Then something must pull it,"
Said Elf number two,
"What about some giraffes?
Or a monkey might do."

"Well," Elf number one said,
He'd note the remark,
But he didn't think either
Could see in the dark.

Then bats were suggested,
But they were turned down,
As their image was bad
For a man about town.

Then someone said "Glow-worms,
They would at least glow."
But they were rejected
As being too slow.

Then one Elf said, "Reindeers
Would perhaps suit the bill,
They could slide down the hills
And do pulling up hill."

The first year we used them
We got round quite well,
And just to please reindeers,
Each one got a bell.

The following year I
Tried out a new trick,
I found going down chimneys
Was mucky, but quick.

Things have not changed a lot
Since that very first night,
Though now folk know I'm coming
Some leave on a light.

And some put out cake
Or perhaps a mince pie,
And as for the drink,
Well, I get rather high.

Some say at my age
Such a journey is mad,
For a man of four hundred
I don't do so bad.

It's a lot of hard work
For just one night a year,
But it's worth it i'n't morning
To hear what I hear.

It's "Mum, look at this"
And "Dad, fix me that",
And I smile to myself
Like a big Cheshire cat.

Then I take off my boots
And I sit by the fire,
And I think to myself
P'raps next year I'll retire.

THREE IN A BED

I was born just before Hitler came into power
And soon after that it was clear
That war was as certain as nose on me face,
And shortages soon would appear.

The first thing they wanted was metal for guns,
So t'Government made a request,
They said will you send us your pots and your pans,
Your bedsteads or p'raps a tin chest.

Me mother, a loyalist down to her bones
Without further ado
Broke up my small cot, which were made out of steel,
And chucked in a saucepan or two.

This were all very fine until bedtime
When it all seemed a bit of a squeeze,
For I had to go in with me mother and dad,
So I slept between elbows and knees.

With only one mattress between us
We managed with three in a bed,
But as I got bigger we slept like sardines
With their feet either side of my head.

At age of eighteen I was drafted
To go and serve country and Queen,
But shortages in the armed forces
Made three in a bed the routine.

At age twenty-one I got married
To a blonde who were leggy and tall,
But our nuptials proved a disaster
For she came with her mother an' all.

Well it fair put a stop to t'proceedings,
For though mother slept over to t'right,
Her teeth in a glass of cold water
Seemed to grin at me all through the night.

She didn't move out till years later
When I kicked up a bit of a fuss,
Then the wife said, "I'm having a baby,
Will you mind if it comes in with us?"

At finish we had seven children,
So I've never had bed to myself,
There were so many sharing at one time
I put two underneath on a shelf.

Me and wife now are into our dotage,
So we're both in a home for the old,
Matron said I can have me own bedroom,
But I don't believe all that I'm told.

I've just seen the news on the telly
And NHS cutbacks are rife,
I just hope if I'm sharing me bed once again
It'll be with a nurse and not wife.

"With only one mattress between us
We managed with three in a bed."

FEELINGS

Let not a hurt of yours be manifold in the market place, neither let your joy overflow in the streets, rather give reverence to these enchanted moments, taking stock of each and measuring them against the weight of time. Some little deed has brought you thus, and you alone hold both the feeling and the balance in your heart.

Share sparingly the inner thoughts you hold with only those most dear, and having imparted them remain to have them reassessed by those who, further from the scene, may offer wiser council and loving honesty.

Great elation and deepest sorrow are but momentary aliens in a common enough earth, yet in the finished tapestry of life give colour on a grander scale than daily threads can offer.

Give heed to nature, remembering that the hardest winter will bring forth the greatest harvest in due season, and yet too great a crop will in its turn become a rotting heap.

Time and time alone will be the arbiter of truth, and even then a truth which has been patched together by mere mortals.

Think then a while upon your deepest feelings and give them their moment. Reach inward and know yourself, for everyone has a strength untapped, a grace unknown, a love divine.

GIVING UP

I'm thinking of giving up women
Though I've only had one in my life,
I was known as a bit of a dandy
When I was engaged to the wife.

We'd only been courting for ten years
When I led my sweetheart down the aisle,
But Deirdre was putty in my hands
When I put on my debonair smile.

She thought me as mild as a kitten,
But I was a bear underneath,
And our romance took off with vengeance
Once I put in my new set of teeth.

People think that I'm stable and settled,
They don't know of my passionate thirst,
So I can't see me giving up women,
I just hope that they give me up first.

I'm thinking of giving up smoking,
I've cut down to just five a day,
Well, I only have one to be honest,
The other four I give away.

I share mine with those in the office
So the expense is really quite small,
You see they've given up altogether
So they don't buy any at all.

I'm thinking of giving up gambling,
It's a habit I really must stop,
Though one time I did join the annual sweep
And my number came up to the top.

I once had a bet on the Derby
But my horse I'm afraid lost a shoe,
So now I'm determined to give up the vice
And I bet you a fiver I do.

I'm going to restrain my bad temper,
I'm inclined to get cross and erupt,
I once stamped my foot at the children
When I thought they were being abrupt.

I'm thinking of giving up drinking,
Though I never have more than just one,
But with buying a round for the others
It's surprising my money's soon gone.

I'm thinking of giving up most things,
Though I might feel a little bereft,
For when I've surrendered my pleasures
There isn't an awful lot left.

So I think I'll give up resolutions,
I'll put all my fine words on the shelf,
I'll smoke and I'll drink and I'll gamble
And really indulge in myself.

And when I've got old and decrepit
And I've got to my three score and ten,
I'll review all my promises made now
And who knows I might make them again.

THE HAIRDO

Don't tell me: you've just had your hair done,
Well I don't really know what to say,
It certainly looks very different,
But just tell me — how much did you pay?

Oh, it's Monday, they did it for half price,
Well you can't expect much for two pound,
If they used that there perming solution
I don't think they'd enough to go round.

Now don't get me wrong, it looks lovely,
It's got fashion and flair I've no doubt,
I'd have the same done myself love,
But I'd not have the guts to walk out.

Mind you, I think fringes are in now,
And they've done it all plaited like lace,
Then they've dyed it and pulled in to one side
Like a curtain hung over your face.

They've gone to some trouble with that piece,
It makes you look proud and aloof:
Sort of done up on top like a beehive,
Then woven just like a thatched roof.

Did they give your creation a title?
You say that it's called "Morning Pride",
Only I would have called it the "Wing Nut",
Now your ears sort of stick out each side.

*"Mind, it's handy for keeping your hat on
If the wind starts to get a bit strong."*

Have they missed this bit just round the back, love?
Or is it supposed to be long?
Mind, it's handy for keeping your hat on
If the wind starts to get a bit strong.

Now you must tell me — who did the styling?
You say it's a fellow called Jim?
Only I might be going next Monday,
And I'll make sure I don't ask for him!

MY CHRISTMAS PAST

How old was I those many Christmases ago? Those frosty, freezing, merry-making Christmases, when mystery and a little apprehension started in late November and oh so slowly reached a laughing, jolly climax that lasted well into the New Year.

The frozen puddles, yes, that was always the first sign that winter was beginning to introduce herself into my little street. Going to school in the dark, my short trousers chafing my chapped legs. My gas mask in a cardboard box over my shoulder, and even as I set out, a wishing I were home again and safe in the well-lit, warm back kitchen behind the shop, that was my winter world. There, I would drive my dinky cars around the pattern on the rug that made roads and fields, and, with a few dominoes and a lot of imagination, a whole world in miniature was laid out before me.

By early December there were secrets to be kept, and hiding places to find where parents wouldn't look. Somewhere like the back of a drawer to hide the bottle of Boots 4711 scent which Mum had mentioned was her favourite only days ago. And Dad's handkerchief, which I never did think was very exciting, but of which he always seemed to enthuse at great length as though it were a treasured gift indeed.

Christmas proper started at school. This entailed making mile upon mile of gummed paper trimmings; these along with more gummed paper lanterns were festooned in a criss-cross manner from the lights until the lamp shades would take no more. All this gaiety of colour never fooled me for one minute into forgetting that I was a daily prisoner in this brown-panelled, glass-partitioned building called "school".

The class party itself was a well-organised affair. Some sensible games, a quiz or two — which always seemed to me an excuse to give another lesson in the guise of fun. And then to finish the festivity: country dancing, accompanied by a wind-up gramophone. I remember "Gathering Peapods" to the sound of a very tinny orchestra, who were obviously playing in someone's bathroom while the tap was still running. However, I always thoroughly enjoyed this activity, as it gave me the opportunity to hold Rita Hatfield and Pat Southall, two nine-year-old beauties whose glamour I couldn't resist, and who may, before the afternoon was out, give me a kiss — though why they always giggled at me when I was so madly in love with them I never did understand.

Being war time, the food for this Christmas bonanza was on an ad hoc basis. It was a case of: bring what you can and eat what there is. Everyone's contribution was put onto a large table and you helped yourself at the appropriate time. Unfortunately, this often resulted in getting someone else's watery jam sandwich instead of the precious egg and cress your mother had so lovingly prepared.

After the party was over, we were all given some of the paper decorations to take home and, suddenly, that was it: school was over and two whole weeks stretched out like eternity before me.

Being basically selfish, like most children my upper-most thoughts were usually on the matter of "What am I to get this year?" I could never understand why people told me that it was better to give than to receive, for while I enjoyed the buying and wrapping up my little gifts for the family, it wasn't to be compared with the far greater delight of receiving presents from others.

Our home was always well dressed for Christmas. We had an artificial tree, which I suppose with hindsight was rather moth-eaten, but to me at the time was of the greenest and grandest proportions. The branches were always carefully opened into the horizontal and then my sister and I would begin the decoration. By the time I was old enough to assist her, most of the beautiful glass baubles were broken, so extra care was taken with the silver and red Father Christmas and the pipe that whis-tled when you blew down it. Even the robin that clipped onto a branch only had one leg, and though the glass bell had lost most if its enamel, at least it still was able to give out a tinkle tinkle if anyone walked on the loose floorboard that shook the sideboard. These few treasured trinkets were augmented by a host of other artefacts which were of the home-made variety, namely bell-shaped milk bottle tops and silver paper angels which at a dis-tance could easily be mistaken for crumpled milk bottle tops. In the centre of our ceiling was an orange and cream mottled lamp shade supported by three chains, just as in school this made an ideal anchor point to hang yet more home-made paper trimmings.

By now cards would start arriving from places one had only heard of and would certainly never visit — Didsbury, Nantwich, Workington, and even one from an uncle in Australia. There was always something exciting about being the one to open one of these greetings, although this was sometimes soon lost in the criticism heaped on the sender for his or her meanness at the size of card chosen.

When Christmas Eve finally arrived, dire warnings were issued about staying awake too long. I was never sure of the mechanics of Father Christmas getting around the world in one night, but instinct told me that I wouldn't be overlooked. Nevertheless, I was usually awake when my sister came to bed some time later, she being seven years my senior and, to me, very old. I don't know what time I awoke Christmas morning, but it was always dark. My mind was usually far more alert than my body, and first question to spring to mind: "Has he been or has he yet to come?" Dare I sit up and fish around or pretend I am still asleep? What if he were to walk in as I was sitting up In bed? Tragedy? The problem was usually resolved by shuffling down the bed clothes and hoping my feet would strike something firm. As this was always the case, my whole concentration and consideration was now the size of the pillow case. Would it be full to the top? Would it be half empty? Would it bulge or be thin? Had Father Christmas brought me what I really wanted or just things I wasn't really bothered about? Or, worst of all worlds, would there be lots of books that were all reading and no pictures? I didn't mind annuals, especially "Film Fun". "Rupert" was always my favourite, for apart from all the bright pictures, I loved the small rhyming story that ran underneath. But please don't let it be "Roy of the Rovers" or "Benjamin and the Bengal Tigers".

I can still smell those early morning presents. They were a beautiful blend of new paint and printer's ink. Even now when I open a new book, I am transported through the years to an early Christmas morning many years ago.

Parties at our home fell into two categories: the relations' party, a formal occasion that may, or may not, end up quite jolly, but there was no guarantee. And then there was the party held for friends when we were sure of a good time: a good sing, and with any luck a game of charades that would go on until very late, and get sillier as the evening progressed. Being a Methodist household, the strongest drink being handed around came out of a teapot, but for the merriment it created, it might have been the strongest of brews. I do remember, however, that the one and only one bottle of sherry or port was purchased to wish everyone the season's greetings sometime during the Christmas festivities.

To prepare for these events, once again the large room upstairs which ran over the shop would be brought into service. This was often a hazardous business as, rather than start a fire in this room with paper and sticks, it was usually the case that my father would take a shovel full of live coals from the living room fire and proceed to walk up the stairs with flames and smoke bellowing out in front of him — the trick being not to set fire to the pile of coats hanging on the back of the door at the foot of the stairs. He was usually closely followed by my mother, who would be right behind him calling out directions — "Gill, mind the door, be careful on the stairs, look at the smoke you're making and I've just cleaned up!" This verbal accompaniment would continue until the coal was placed safely in the grate.

The room itself, not having been heated since the previous Christmas, was usually only a degree or two above freezing, so a day's coal was carefully rationed out to get this icebox into a warm and socially acceptable place. Still more gummed paper chains were the order of the day, though in later years more sophisticated bought ones were hoisted, and these along with a real tree were so delightful and exciting as to set a small boy into sleepless nights for the duration of the season.

Fairy lights were unobtainable at this time of early post war and most homes, while still having the wiring and fittings, were unable to buy the bulbs which had burned out during the previous wartime Christmases. My dad, however, connected a string of small coloured bedside lamp bulbs and these made a great show, although I imagine they must have put quite a strain on the tree, as well as our old fuse box in the cellar. No matter, it was Christmas and only the best was good enough.

Christmases past mix and merge into a potpourri of joviality and warmth. A rich receipt of laughing uncles, who with any luck would take me on one side and give me half a crown. Of well-proportioned aunties who carried an entire drawer full of jewellery about them, as *if it had rained glass beads and pearls the length of their journey to see us. All this was hung around a well-rouged face and a hairstyle that had been recently ironed into a perm.*

Sometimes, just sometimes, a sound of music, a smell of newness, a phrase spoken and I am once again transported into that yesteryear of trust and innocence, of warmth and love, that was for me as a child a very Happy Christmas.

JUST ANOTHER DAY
(A Widow's Story)

It's just another day, you know,
I've nothing much to do,
I'll p'raps go up and down the shops
To pass an hour or two.

And yet it seems like yesterday
I'd shop for John and Jane,
And the house was full of laughter
When I hurried back again.

There was purpose then for going
With the family to keep,
But now it's just as though the house
Has fallen fast asleep.

John's quite a somebody these days,
His job takes him away,
He's a lovely house and garden,
Though I've never been to stay.

He says he'll come and see me
But I know he's plenty on,
Last time he came, he stayed an hour
Before his time was gone.

And Jane's a ballet dancer now,
I've not seen her for years,
But she sends me lovely postcards
From wherever she appears.

She's travelled all around the world
And danced before the Queen,
And I'd love to go and see her
But of course I've never been.

Well, they say it costs a fortune
In them theatres these days,
And I haven't got enough for that
On what my pension pays.

I only wish her dad was here,
He'd be so proud you know,
He gave up smoking cigarettes
To pay for her to go.

It's a shame the way they grow up
But they've got their lives to lead,
It seems so short a time before
They leave home to succeed.

I sometimes wonder if they know
How dear they are to me,
Why, there's not a day goes by
When I don't think of all the three.

I try not to get maudlin
For I've had my share of life,
The good days and the bad days,
Some happiness and strife.

And thinking on, there's plenty more
A lot worse off than me,
So I fill my days with business
And breaks for cups of tea.

It's been a good life after all,
Some sunshine and some rain,
And if I had my time to come
I'd do it all again.

THE TRAIN JOURNEY

The weather was just lovely
So I pinched a day or two,
And I thought I'd take a short break
To a town just outside Crewe.

I'd read about the adverts
That said "Mini hols by train"
So I went down to the booking place
To let them take the strain.

I'd not been near the station
For a good ten years or so,
But the same familiar voice announced
The trains were running slow.

The odd policeman standing round
Looked smaller than before,
But I recognised the porters
Throwing boxes on the floor.

I walked to one and asked him
If he'd tell me where to book,
He said, "Try the booking office."
And he gave me such a look.

So I tried to open several doors
All painted sooty brown
Till I found one with a handle
That was put on upside down.

I struggled for some moments
Till the handle came away,
But as it did the door revealed
The place I had to pay.

I entered with the handle
Closely gripped in my right hand,
And hoped the station booking man
Would kindly understand.

"Excuse me," I said timidly
Beginning to explain,
"I seem to have your door knob,
Shall I put it back again?"

He said, "You must be joking,
What you've done is really fine,
It will stop folk coming in to book
And taking up our time."

I soldiered on and spoke up
In a voice quite loud and clear:
"I require a return ticket."
He said, "Where?" I said, "Back here."

"It would help sir," he said tersely,
"If you could give us lads a clue
As to where your destination is."
I said, "Just outside Crewe."

"I entered with the handle
Closely gripped in my right hand."

He continued with his questions
By first asking me what day
I was thinking of departing
For my little trip away.

I thought this rather personal,
So asked him "Why the quiz?"
He said, "I've forms to fill in,
Well, you know just how it is."

Then he went on to inform me
Of the rules which now apply,
He said, "If you want to travel
British Rail want to know why."

"Then there's all these coloured tickets
For the different times of day,
'Cause if you start at midnight
You'll not have as much to pay.

"And of course you can get cheaper
Though the seating's pretty hard,
If you don't mind going parcel post
And sitting with the guard.

"But for just a little extra cash
You could just book a seat,
But that doesn't guarantee
You won't be standing on your feet.

"Then there's Mondays and there's Wednesdays
When it takes a long detour,
So we have to charge you extra
'Cause you're on another hour.

"Now Thursday's always cheaper
So you might find that a boon,
But of course it's half-day closing
So we stop the trains at noon.

"What about a season ticket
For a weekly to and fro?
And if you didn't like it,
Well, you wouldn't have to go.

"Of course the weekend's not the time
To travel anywhere,
You see Harry in the signal box
Goes home and no one's there."

By this time I was speechless,
But not wanting any fuss
I just closed the door behind me
And I went to catch the bus.

HOLIDAY WEAK
(A Little Advice from the Good Lady Wife)

Just when are you fetching a brochure?
You promised to go yesterday,
I've only to look at a holiday book
And "Cleethorpes" is all you can say.

We have this to-do every April,
We always fall out and cross swords,
I mentioned a trip to some place in a ship
And you booked a canoe on the Broads.

We had the same arguments last year
When I said that I wanted to fly,
All you could suggest, as you sat in your vest,
Was "Let's give hang gliding a try."

And look at our honeymoon fortnight
When you told all the guests what you'd spent,
You announced to the crowds we'd soon be in the clouds
And we went up Mam Tor in a tent.

You told me one year that you'd fly me
To some paradise island by night,
Then I woke up at dawn to a noisy fog horn
And found we were in't Isle of Wight.

And don't think I've forgotten that Easter
When you said that my mum could come too,
When she said, "Shall I see anyone who knows me?"
You said, "Yes, when we get to the zoo."

You'll do anything just to save money,
You're as mean as a country church mouse,
It was you booked that spree, with electric all free,
And we finished up in a lighthouse.

And remember that caravan fortnight,
You said we'd tour up dale and hill,
But you like a clown booked a van bolted down
And we had to spend two weeks in Rhyl.

My parents warned me you were careful,
I know now what my mother meant,
I've only to look what you've ringed in the book:
"Come strawberry picking in Kent".

I think best thing to do is go separate,
I'll try somewhere exciting and new,
While you spend the week in your bed fast asleep
'Cause that's what you usually do.

THE CAR LOT

Salesman   Good afternoon sir, can I help you?
                  I can see you're a man of good taste,
                  You're probably up from the city
                  So you'll not have much time left to waste.

                  I'll get straight to the point, you've
                        dropped lucky,
                  You've spotted the bargain I see,
                  That car has had one lady owner
                  And she cried when she sold it to me.

Browser   Well really I'm just on my lunch break
                  So I'm only just browsing around,
                  The car that I've got is a good one —
                  A bit noisy, but really quite sound.

Salesman   Is that it parked up on the highway?
                  I should move it along were I you,
                  It could easy get taken away sir,
                  On Tuesdays the bin men are due.

Browser   I was hoping I might part exchange it,
                  It looks good when it's polished you know.

Salesman   The last time I saw one of those sir
                  It appeared on the Antiques Road Show.

Salesman   Now to get back to this bargain offer,
                      I'd make more profit selling a pram,
                      I've marked it too cheap I can see now,
                      But that's just the chap that I am.

Browser   I ought to let my wife look round it,
                      Though she's really not bothered what kind,
                      She does like the back seat to be comfy
                      Just so she can nag from behind.

Salesman   Now look sir I'll do you a favour,
                      You'll have noticed the back wheels are flat,
                      Well, I'll throw in a couple of tyres,
                      Now I just can't say fairer than that.

Browser   Is this mileage correct on the meter?
                      It says 3,000 miles, that's not much,
                      Yet the seats are right through to the
                            springing
                      And the pedal's worn out on the clutch.

Salesman   Well, the old lady was on the big side
                      And her wooden leg wore that away,
                      She was injured while fighting the war sir,
                      That's the truth, now what more can I say?

Browser   Do you mind if I just think it over?
                      I don't want to do anything rash,
                      I'll p'raps bring the wife back to see it,
                      Now I'm sorry, I really must dash.

Salesman Well you know how to drive a hard bargain,
But let's face it you've beaten me down,
Just don't tell your pals what I've offered,
Or my name will be mud in this town.

Browser I don't really know how to put this:
I just don't want your car, to be blunt,
Your story was good, but for one thing:
You've left "TAXI" still stuck on the front.

THE SUPERMARKET

I think I'll just pop down to Tesco
To get something nice for our tea,
I'll see what they've got
'Cause we don't want a lot —
Just something for mother and me.

I daren't let her loose on her own there,
She buys everything in the store,
I'll just get what we need
Then she'll have to concede
That I can pay far less for more.

I'll just take a pound of these apples
And these oranges look rather nice,
And I really can't miss
Seedless grapes sweet as this
Especially for sale at this price.

"Buy three tins of beans for a discount",
Well, I'd best take advantage of that,
If we don't eat them now
They'll get used up somehow
We can always just give them the cat.

The smell of that bread is delicious,
I'll just take a new loaf and some scones,
And these chops look OK
For our dinner Sunday
And on Monday we'll stew up the bones.

I've been meaning to get one of these things
But that tool shop is miles from our place,
A screwdriver and drill and some white polyfil,
And I think I'll splash out on a brace.

What's this? Oh, some new fizzy drink stuff,
Go on then, I'll give it a try,
Good Heavens, my trolley's collapsing,
And so many things I could buy.

I've still not got what I came in for:
Something nice we can have for our tea,
P'raps some sardines on toast seem to fit the bill most,
Though that chocolate ice cream would suit me.

My, just look at those liquorice allsorts,
I'll treat myself just to a pound,
And some turkish delight (we can eat those tonight),
Or save them till company comes round.

Hello love, I'm back from the shopping,
It's not taken me long to get round,
I've got something for tea that will suit you and me
And I've only spent forty-eight pounds!

UP MARKET

I don't wish to brag, but we're posh now
'Cause we moved house just six months ago,
And I'm learning a whole different language
Which I'll tell you in case you don't know.

We've a "studio" up on the third floor
Which looks like an attic to me,
And the sun shines in straight through the "fan light"
Which is right where the window would be.

Then you come down a floor to the landing,
Or I should say the "upstairs corridor"
Where there's doors leading off into bedrooms,
Only they're not the same as before.

The back room we keep all the junk in
Is the "guest room" — now aren't you impressed?
But what with the mortgage repayments
I doubt it will see any guests.

The box room is more of a cupboard,
It's just at the end of the hall,
Well that's now been renamed the "maid's room",
But by gum, "maid" will have to be small.

The front bedroom is large and palatial
With all the requirements en suite,
There's a bath and a shower in the toilet
And a basin that washes your feet.

On the ground floor of course that's all different,
I don't really know where to begin,
For a start I don't hang my clothes on a nail,
We've a cupboard to put our coats in.

We had a front room at the old house,
A nice enough place in its way,
But people in these parts don't have one,
So we sit in the "lounge" with the bay.

The back room we spend most of our time in,
But in one corner now there's a mat,
And that's called the "dining room area",
So we all eat our meals stood on that.

We've a "patio" where the back yard was
And the grass beyond that is the "grounds",
The railings are now the "perimeter fence"
And my whippets have been changed to hounds.

The sideboard is renamed the "bureau"
And the "chaise longue" has replaced the settee,
We eat "gateau" which used to be sponge cake
And drink Earl Grey and not Typhoo tea.

My pullover's gone to the jumble
I now wear a waistcoat instead,
I've a suit with plus fours I go out in
With a deerstalker stuck on my head.

The wife who wore flannelette nighties
Now puts on some "French lingerie",
And she comes up to bed in a face pack,
She looks better like that I must say.

Pyjamas have replaced my nightshirt
And I'm learning to be upper class,
My beaker has gone from my bedside
And I keep my teeth now in a glass.

Our lives are just one long engagement
With society people we chat,
We'd like to go hunting and fishing
But in Heeley there's not much of that.

These changes are all most confusing
It's a new world to me I might say,
The only thing that's the same are the neighbours —
Well, we've only moved three doors away.

ILL FEELINGS

I've been very poorly just lately,
In truth, I've been near to death's door,
I couldn't just name the affliction,
But I don't want it back anymore.

It started last Friday at teatime
And I thought to myself, "What a burke!
Why can't I feel bad on a Monday?
Then at least I could have time off work."

To begin with my eyes started running,
And I'd sneeze every now and again,
My throat felt all dry and was burning,
And my nose got as blocked as a drain.

I went round to the pub for some company,
And met up with a long-standing pal,
I said, "What would you do with my symptoms?"
And he said, "Chuck yourself in't canal."

He drank up, then got up and left me,
So I sat on my own, feeling low,
Then I went round to chat with some others,
But surprisingly, they had to go.

This set me a bit of a problem:
Should I tell other people or not?
If there's one thing that makes you feel better,
It's telling your friends what you've got.

I was no better Saturday morning,
But the wife said, "I think you'll pull through,
I had the same thing all last weekend
But I never told any of you."

I thought I'd best go to the doctor's,
After all, that's what they're there for,
So I sat in the waiting room waiting
And read about winning the war.

I explained to the doctor my symptoms
And his face looked all puzzled and vague,
He said, "You've got some sort of an ailment
That's a cross between mumps and the plague."

He wrote me lengthy prescription
That just looked like Latin to me,
The chemist said, "No need to worry,
At your age you'll get it all free."

He gave me a carton of tablets
Which read, "Take two before you retire",
Well, I've ten years to go till I'm sixty
So I went home and chucked them on't fire.

On Sunday I coughed and I spluttered,
I thought I was breathing me last,
I slumped on the settee and kept gasping
Every time anybody walked past.

My family are hard and unthinking,
But the wife went a little too far,
She said, "Get up and stop overacting,
You're taking us out in the car."

How I got through that day is a wonder,
But somehow I managed to cope,
I know if I went back to't doctor's
He'd tell me I hadn't a hope.

The next day you wouldn't believe it,
I woke up as fit a flea.
The wife said, "Get working, it's Monday."
And I replied, "Aye, it would be."

I rose, washed and shaved and had breakfast
Then set off to work on the bus,
And as I sat there I was thinking,
It's a good job I don't make a fuss.

GOING GREEN

A man on the wireless was saying
How the balance of nature has changed,
And the only way now to reverse it
Is to get all our lives re-arranged.

So I started this week to be different
And to think before making a move,
Will my actions do more untold damage
Or start to make matters improve?

So I cook everything on a coal fire,
The oven's redundant these days,
Now I'm not using gas or electric
I can burn things in dozens of ways.

My car is parked up in the garage,
Now my bicycle's out on the street,
The trouble is now when I get into work
I'm practically dead on my feet.

I use insect repellant that's friendly
'Cause the world's ozone layer's getting thin,
And the flies are so pleased that I use it
They fair chuck themselves at the tin

My garden's been transformed just lately,
I'm just using natural manure,
I seem to have lost all my friends though,
But why that's occurred I'm not sure.

My rhubarb is coming up lovely
And turnips just have to be seen,
But aphids have eaten my roses
So most of my garden's just green.

I save my glass jars when they're empty
And take them all back to the store,
But it's put me right off buying strawberry jam,
Well, you don't know who's had it before.

Then there's acid rain causing a problem,
So it's best to go out when it's fine,
And that's why umbrellas aren't lasting as long
And going in holes all the time.

"Now I'm not using gas or electric
I can burn things in dozens of ways."

We now use recycled loo paper
Hung on the lavatory door,
But I think that the roll that we're using
Was wedding confetti before.

I've stopped smoking to help with pollution
And with all other bad habits I strive,
And if I were truthful about it
I'd be far better dead than alive.

PARTY TIME

We've just thrown a marvellous party,
We invited the Queen and her heirs,
We asked Charles and Di, I don't really know why
'Cause they never asked us to theirs.

They replied to our kind invitation
On tissue-like paper, so thin,
They wrote just to say they were busy that day
And that evening they'd like a night in.

The invites were beautifully written
With our old family crest done in silk,
Then we wrote at the end, "Bring a bottle, good friend",
Now we'll never drink all of that milk.

Mrs Thatcher made silly excuses
Though she said they were matters profound,
Some furniture change she was going to arrange:
She was moving her cabinet round.

But Neil Kinnock came with his missus,
So he gave a Welsh touch to the do,
But he stood up to speak and he asked for a leek
So I showed him the way to the loo.

My missus laid on quite a banquet,
We had sausages, bubble and squeak,
Our grandma came back for three helpings
And her funeral is next Tuesday week.

Uncle Horace just ate mashed potatoes
Though he said he'd not had any lunch,
With a tear in his eye he told us just why
For he'd lost his false teeth in the punch.

After supper was over we played games
But they didn't cause much of a stir,
We all put on a mask and then had the task
Of trying to guess who we were.

The wife did her usual striptease,
She thought it would turn the men on,
Then she struck up a pose as she took off her clothes
And the men shouted, "Put them back on!"

And then we all played famous people,
Uncle John's "Fred Astaire" cut a dash,
Then Aunt Edie came dressed as Hitler again
'Cause she already has the moustache.

In a mini skirt Maureen played cello,
A piece that was called "Maiden Prayer",
All the men shouted "More" and "Let's hear an encore"
'Cause she showed all her black underwear.

Uncle Jack did a trick with some money:
He pretended to swallow a pound,
Then Mary Malone tried the trick on her own
And that money's never been found.

Little Kevin played hours on the piano,
Just the one tune he knew, "Three Blind Mice",
But he stopped what he did when the big piano lid
Accidentally fell on him — twice!

Auntie Violet whose voice is soprano
In Vera Lynn's songs got immersed,
She sang "We'll meet again, don't know where, don't
          know when",
And I thought, "Not if I see you first."

We've just thrown a marvellous party
With food, drink and musical sounds,
Though it cost quite a lot for the pleasures we got
It was worth every bob of ten pounds.

WELCOME HOME
(A Homecoming Greeting from the Dear Wife)

What time of the night do you call this?
You said you were just popping out.
You've been gone for ages and spent all your wages
And come back here smelling of stout.

And don't think I don't know what you're up to,
You're not fooling me with that look,
You can't keep much from me that I don't want to see,
I can read your face just like a book.

When you went out of here you were dressed up,
You'd a trilby, a coat and a stick,
Now your face is all pink, you look far worse for drink
And your hat says "Come on, kiss me quick".

Well I've just had enough, I can tell you,
The dog's more affection than you,
I'm not keen on his breath, but he licks me to death,
Which is more that I'm getting from you.

And what do you mean, you've been working?
Well I don't believe that, to be blunt,
'Cause whatever it's worth, there's no job on earth
Where you put trousers on back to front.

You've been out with the lads for an hour
And that's how your money's got spent,
Well, which fellow's the one who had black stockings on
And wears that unique smelling scent?

And just look at the state you've come home in!
If the neighbours have seen you I'll die,
You've one shoe that's gone and you've no collar on,
And you've lipstick all over your tie.

Have you looked at the time? It's ten thirty!
Most people are home and in bed,
And don't try to kid me: you went out before tea
Saying, "I'll just nip out for some bread."

Well I blame your parents for this lot,
Your mother was always half tight,
When she drank madeira you couldn't get near her,
She'd hit anybody in sight.

You were drunk on the day we were married,
Goodness knows why I ever chose you,
When that vicar cried, "Will you take this fair bride?"
You said, "Yes, well I think that she'll do."

You ought to just look in the mirror,
And you'd give up the drink out of fear,
You've got one black eye and I don't know just why
You've a pork pie stuck out of your ear.

Well, don't think you're sleeping in my bed,
You're not breathing fumes over me,
I'll get the camp bed, you can sleep there instead
Or go downstairs on the settee.

Just step inside where I can see you
And don't wear your boots on this floor,
Now this can't be right, now you're into the light
I can see you're the man from next door.

"And don't think I don't know what you're up to,
You're not fooling me with that look."

AT YOUR SERVICE

Are you giving your engine a tune-up?
They're tricky are them to put right.
I once had a grommett come loose on that sort
And I swear I was up half the night.

Did you buy it from him round the corner?
Well you'd best not go back to complain,
The chap down the road took his car in
And he's never been heard of again.

And that guarantee is worth nothing,
It says that if anything's wrong
You're to take the car back to the builder —
And that model's made in Hong Kong.

Course you've slipped up by getting the "C" range,
They only made fifty that style,
They put in a new carburettor
And they only do ten to the mile.

Is that wheel supposed to be different?
It's just that the car seems to lean,
It says "Nissan" on three of your hub caps,
And this one it says "Walls' Ice Cream".

Have you noticed it pulling to one side?
You've seized up your brakes, I'll be bound,
Only just as you pulled in the driveway
You'd only three wheels going round.

I should check it for oil when you've finished,
You might find you're needing some more,
I don't think there's much in your engine,
See, most of it's here on the floor.

It's not much use pulling that starter,
Your battery's gone flat I can see,
And it's no good you asking the question,
What shape do I think it should be?

I think you'd best get the AA out,
They say that they're good at repairs,
Oh I see now the vehicle is yellow,
Don't tell me! This is one of theirs!

SALE AWAY!

I've been to the sales for a bargain
And you'll never guess just what I've bought,
Some people go silly and buy willy-nilly
But I've made sure that I wasn't caught.

It's surprising the things that's on offer
When you've plenty of time to shop round,
Now my neighbour reckons the goods are all seconds
But just look at the things that I've found.

I bet you've not got one of these things:
It's an opener for bottles that stick,
When a lid won't come off or a screw top is tough
This gadget will soon do the trick.

And the best is the price that it's cost me,
It was marked up a pound I could see,
But they'd stuck on a sticker to clear the lot quicker
And reduced them to 99p.

Oh, and then I went over to dresses
But most of them there were too tight,
But I found one too large so they said for a charge
That they're going to make it just right.

This teasmaid was on special offer
And really it's just what I need,
The teapot won't work and the clock goes berserk
But the lamp will be handy to read.

And just look at these shoes that I'm wearing:
They're a little bit tight to be sure,
I got there just too late so they hadn't an eight
But they'd plenty of these, they're size four.

"It's surprising the things
that's on offer
When you've plenty of time
to shop round."

I've got six pairs of tights from the market,
They were free if you bought two men's shirts,
There's no gusset in some and in others no bum
But no matter I'll wear longer skirts.

I've a trouser press now in my bedroom,
Well the man said, "Buy this for your spouse."
Now I should have refused, it will never get used
'Cause of course I've no man in the house.

I sometimes think, is it all worth it?
All that pushing and shoving I've braved,
But I know I've done right when I get home at night
And think of the money I've saved.

LATE KICK-OFF

I'll not shout down again, "Are you coming?"
You said you'd be straight after me,
If you don't come I'm putting the light out
Then you'll bang your toes, just wait and see.

I'm not surprised you don't feel tired,
You've spent more hours asleep than our cat,
Your eyes never opened till Match of the Day
But you managed to wake up for that.

It was just the same when we got married,
I'll never forget that first night,
I went up to bed all excited
And you stayed up to watch the big fight.

I don't know I'm sure what your game is,
You've always put sport before me,
On our honeymoon I mentioned "Let's play around"
And we finished up on the first tee.

And now we get cricket all summer,
And it's, "Make sure my whites are all clean."
I wouldn't mind if you were playing
But you only make tea for the team.

When you've finished with cricket, it's snooker,
According to you you're a pro,
Why they made you reserve for the YMCA
When you say you're so good I don't know.

Of course then it's Wimbledon fortnight,
Your boss must suspect something queer,
You must be the only chap working
Whose grandmother dies every year.

Then it's "forty–love", "match play" and "new ball",
You watch every game like a fool,
And I just can't get round with me hoover
With you sat there on that high stool.

And you know it all when you watch ski-ing:
"It's as easy as having a bath."
Course you didn't say that last December
When you slipped down just sweeping the path.

You waste all your money on horses,
You've always bet over the top,
I remember the day that you started
Mr Ladbroke had one corner shop.

And you don't seem to mind losing money,
At the boat race you wasn't deterred,
You must be the only man living
Who backed Oxford the year they came third.

Then of course you're an expert on football,
Well, you are when watching the TV,
Mind the last time you did any dribbling
Was when you were eating your tea.

That reminds me, just check the back door's locked
Before you make tracks up to bed,
Good grief is it that time already?
I'd best come down for breakfast instead.

THE NAVIGATOR

You should have turned left at that junction
Where it said "All diversions this way",
See: now we've turned onto a trunk road,
We could be here best part of the day.

Well look, take the third turning your side,
That should get us back to this town,
No, I tell a lie, I mean my side,
I'm reading the map upside down.

You should see coming up a church steeple
And then there's a wood, so go slow,
If we've not passed a toilet before then
You'd best stop, I'll just have to go.

Now turn left, turn left! Now you've missed it,
Well I know that I left it till late,
But I can't do so many jobs, can I?
And I must get me lipstick on straight.

There's a pull-in ahead so we'll stop there,
Let's take in a bit of the view,
What do you mean "It's not worth it"?
I've spent forty years looking at you.

I suppose you could do the job better
Like last year when we went to Heathrow,
You were that busy bragging you'd found a straight road,
How that plane missed us I'll never know.

And another thing while we're about it,
If you loved me you'd do a U-turn,
The wind's coming straight in at my side
And you know that I've just had a perm.

It's high time you bought a new road map,
You've had this old book for an age,
Ignore the church steeple I mentioned,
It's a staple that's holding the page.

You're driving too fast, do you know that?
And that fool behind's trying to pass,
Look, he's flashing his lights to attract you,
I can see his blue lamp in the glass.

I hate navigating these journeys,
It's a job that I'd far rather shelve,
Next time you don't know where you're going
You'll have to find Sainsbury's yourself.

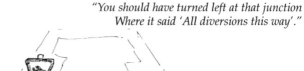

"You should have turned left at that junction
Where it said 'All diversions this way'."